Through the Gateways of a Garden

This book is dedicated to John, Gary and David, without whose persistent encouragement it would never have been written.

Through the Gateways of a Garden

Exploring faith and the environment

Chris Polhill

wild goose
publications

www.ionabooks.com

Copyright © Chris Polhill 2024

First published 2024 by
Wild Goose Publications
Suite 9, Fairfield
1048 Govan Road, Glasgow G51 4XS, Scotland
A division of Iona Community Trading CIC
Limited Company Reg. No. SC156678
www.ionabooks.com

ISBN 978-1-80432-342-7

Cover photo © Chris Polhill

All rights reserved. Apart from the circumstances described below relating to non-commercial use, no part of this publication may be reproduced in any form or by any means, including photocopying or any information storage or retrieval system, without written permission from the publisher via PLSclear.com.

Non-commercial use:
The material in this book may be used non-commercially for worship and group work without written permission from the publisher. If photocopies of sections are made, please make full acknowledgement of the source, and report usage to CLA or other copyright organisation.

Chris Polhill has asserted her right in accordance with the Copyright, Designs and Patents Act, 1988, to be identified as the author of this work.

Overseas distribution
Australia: Willow Connection Pty Ltd, 1/13 Kell Mather Drive,
Lennox Head NSW 2478
New Zealand: Pleroma, Higginson Street, Otane 4170,
Central Hawkes Bay

Printed in the UK by Page Bros (Norwich) Ltd

Contents

Commendation   7
How we came to create the gardens   9
The journey round the gardens   18

The Garden of the Loving Creator   19
The environmental idea in the Garden of the Loving Creator   25
The thinking behind the Garden of the Loving Creator   29

The Garden of the Loved and Forgiven Sinner   35
The environmental idea in the Garden of the Loved
    and Forgiven Sinner   41
The thinking behind the Garden of the Loved and Forgiven Sinner   46

The Discipleship Garden   53
The environmental idea in the Discipleship Garden   60
The thinking behind the Discipleship Garden   64

The Passion Garden   69
The environmental idea in the Passion Garden   74
The thinking behind the Passion Garden   79
The tomb area   85

The Resurrection Garden   87
The environmental idea in the Resurrection Garden   95
The thinking behind the Resurrection Garden   100

Comments from the Gardens visitors' book   110
Prayer   112

Appendix   113
Next steps: An environmental action activity
    for church groups   114

Acknowledgements   121
Notes   122

Commendation

This book is a veritable feast. It tells the story of the pilgrimage garden which Christine and John Polhill have created at Beaudesert on Cannock Chase. It serves as an imaginative guide by explaining the layout of each part of the garden and its symbolism. And it offers an invitation to faith and environmental commitment.

The garden is a kind of horticultural *Pilgrim's Progress*, in which the journey of the Christian life is modelled on the major themes of the Gospel story: the Loving Creator, the Loved and Forgiven Sinner, Discipleship, the Passion Garden and the Tomb, and the Resurrection Garden. Each of these sections is linked with an environmental theme, and with aspects of the Ignatian Spiritual Exercises. Together, the garden and book offer a highly accessible theological and spiritual education, opening new windows of perception on to prayer, our lifestyles and the great questions of life. A visit should be a 'must' for Confirmation candidates in the Midlands.

In his Encyclical Letter *Laudato Si'* Pope Francis has challenged the world to recognise the connection between the environmental crisis and the spiritual hunger that creates so much waste. Environmental responsibility, he says, is not an optional extra, but an integral part of Christian discipleship. This garden and book embody that vision, invite us to explore it, and offer spiritual wisdom and practical ways forward on the journey.

It has been my privilege to know John and Christine over the years in which this great work of theirs has matured, and it is with the same sense of admiration and enthusiasm that I warmly commend this book.

Bishop Michael Bourke,
The first patron of the gardens

Gateways

As I look back
I see the gateways
in life's journey.
Being born, the firstborn,
a gateway making parents –
me to breathing, knowing love;
siblings, East End, school
and all the rest. Leading to

the present moment.
You'll have your own –
thresholds turning tables,
a portal to a different way,
an unexpected growing
and all the norms. Leading to

this chance to read;
to wander through gateways
of faith's footpaths, in a garden.
You are welcome.

How we came to create the gardens

Our gardens are on the southern edge of Cannock Chase in Staffordshire, a place neither John nor I knew or had visited, but when you try to follow God surprising things happen.

Near the end of 1992 we went for a walk in the woods not far from our home in St Albans. It had been a tough year: two of our three children were life-threateningly ill, the women-as-priests issue had made my work difficult as colleagues reacted with what we deacons came to call 'gut lag'. At the time I was a deacon in the C of E, hoping that the priesthood would be open to women before long, hoping to be a vicar some day because General Synod had recently voted in favour of women becoming priests. However I could not see how any of this could come together.

Christmas came, with the worst of the family storm past, but leaving us feeling hopeless and exhausted. As we walked with our two sons, John and I talked a little of the uncle whose death a year before had triggered part of the family trauma. We were also talking about our concerns for the environment, and I just said that I would like to plant trees with the money that my uncle had left us. We then had one of those inspiring moments – as if the Holy Spirit was suddenly among us – and we bubbled with ideas: to plant the trees in a way that said something about God; to have a campsite; a creative workshop place where artists of different skills would work … and these life-giving ideas sparkled in the dead feelings we had inside. Our sons contributed ideas and were excited too; maybe this could be a project that inspired different generations. Hope and new life began to refresh us.

Back at home John excitedly drew up a plan and we discussed possibilities. I knew that the church owned numerous pieces of land (the old glebe land which used to support the parish priest), of which some were small pieces no longer viable in modern farming. So I studied maps where the glebe land was shown, with the objective of creating wildlife corridors, and talked over our ideas with the Archdeacon. There were some small pieces in different parishes that were regarded as possible, and over the next year I visited them, one in the company of an encouraging bishop, and in one of them we did cause hedges to be planted. The difficulty of carrying out any of our ideas, however, was convincing others of the benefits when I was someone who lived outside their parish. One group talked enthusiastically about the piece of land under discussion, but then suggested a number of surveys that needed to be carried out first. We are so good as humans at resisting possible change, often in the guise of concern. Environmental issues are particularly subject to this as changes can set off unexpected consequences. So surveys are not unreasonable, but they are effective in slowing down or preventing change. It also became clear to me from these visits that unless the vicar of the parish concerned was enthusiastic about the idea, nothing would happen.

Concurrently with this exploration we had written to every diocese that had plans for a Community Forest. This was the early 1990s when the government caused twelve Community Forests to be created. The idea was that the new planting would be 'lungs' for the big city areas, and bring new life to the places where they were to be established. The scheme relied on the landowners in the areas being willing to add trees, and also developed derelict and brownfield sites as areas of woodland with public access. The C of E was one of those landowners.

Three dioceses replied to our letter: one was not interested, one we went to see but the diocesan officer was clearly uninterested, and one sent the Social Responsibility Officer (SRO) to see us. He was excited about our ideas and encouraged us to explore possibilities in the Lichfield diocese. We went to the diocese and met both the SRO and the Director of the Community Forest. He arranged for us to be shown round, and to visit different places, just to see the opportunities.

At home reality set in. I was unpaid by the church for the work I did, and we could not afford for John to retire from his well-paid job in London. We did complicated sums, endlessly discussed living standards and their costs, and John had a spreadsheet of where his pension scheme needed to reach for him to retire early. To encourage ourselves John drew a map of what our ideas could look like. There was a woodland of course, with different areas expressing different moods, a campsite, and huts for various crafts. I would look at the map and think, 'For how long will the trees just be sticks surrounded by a tree guard?'

Sixteen months later I was ordained as a priest in the Church of England, and a few months after that I had a house-for-duty post as priest in charge in the small Hertfordshire villages of Cottered and Throcking. We both hoped that this would be a place where we could put our ideas into practice. It was a somewhat naive, 'towny' hope. As a new vicar in a farming area I was on a learning curve, but delighted to be there. This was prime farming land, not the poorer-quality land that woodland is planted on.

Naturally we talked of our ideas, and one or two people did offer us small plots of land to plant up, but nothing like the scale we had in mind at the time. Also, oddly, there was no nudge from the Holy Spirit to do so. We did give some creative expression to our ideas by making large, permanent Easter gardens in the churchyards for which I was responsible, and making 'faith and nature trails' between the churches. Underlining my previous difficulty of trying to do things in churches I was not attached to, I could not persuade other local clergy to join in.

Within a few years John's pension model met the standard-of-living point we had agreed and he took early retirement. He took some space to wind down from the hectic pace of systems design work, did two part-time forestry courses, and then started to look about for ways to bring the project into reality. I expected this to take at least five years, but within six months John had found the site at Beaudesert, on the edge of Cannock Chase in Staffordshire, and we had sold our house in St Albans and bought Little Hayes. It was as if God had created a highway and everything came together. A very different plan had emerged of realising our ideas in a garden that was already in established woodland. It was next door to a large campsite run for young people, mostly in the Guiding and Scouting movement. We also planned to plant trees on a five-acre site that was managed by the Forest of Mercia.

I was in a quandary though. By then I had another village church, St Laurence Ardeley, added to my care (plus a welcome half stipend) and I had really not been in the role long enough. Yet, the vision that brought us there in the first place was pulling us now in a different direction. After much prayer I laid a 'fleece' before God. When a particular pastoral situation in which I was involved was resolved, I would see it as time to move on.

So we came to Little Hayes in the Cannock Chase Area of Outstanding Natural Beauty (AONB), but near areas where coal mines had been and the land was being reclaimed. With people from the church at Heath Hayes we did indeed plant up the five acres of land, but this showed us how limiting it might have been to work with the Community Forest. On the Heath Hayes site we had no choice of either species or design. In our own garden we could do as we liked. From the beginning, even when there was still earth-moving and mud and only small parts of the design visible, people came to look round and see what we were doing. Mothers' Union members were particularly encouraging and they would walk round and tell us where we needed posts for people to hold on to.

We ended up owning Little Hayes for just over a year before we moved in. We had paid for help with the design of the gardens through our membership in the Henry Doubleday Research Association. We talked through our ideas with the garden designers (Mr and Mrs Boaler), and gave them a long list of themes we wanted to incorporate. They persuaded us to abandon the idea of a central garden area that other areas would open out from. Instead they suggested a pathway winding around the space, so that it formed a mini-pilgrimage. This concept has become a key element in visitors' experience of the gardens.

The great value of the Boalers' outline plan was that it enabled us to do some of the clearing and hedge-planting during the year before we moved. Hedges are used to separate the garden areas, and we were hoping to give them a year's extra growth before we moved in. However, although we had put rabbit-netting around the whole space to form the gardens, three rabbits remained inside and ate more than a year's growth on the young hedging plants before we managed to catch them and put them outside our barrier. I wish rabbits would stick to the contract and just eat grass, but they like a varied diet, just as we do, so to have a garden we have needed to keep them out of the cultivated spaces.

The rabbit-netting round the edge of the garden and round each garden area (to contain the ones that will get in anyway!) has inevitably led to a number of gates to pass through from one area to another. This gave me the idea for the book's title, because it symbolises the way that a pilgrimage often opens up barriers within ourselves. I am also fascinated by thresholds, where you are between one space and another. We followed the design that Mr and Mrs Boaler created for us, but transferring from a flat piece of paper to a piece of ground is an interesting experience. We developed the practice of working out the design on a section of beach when we were on holiday. Using stones, seaweed, shells, etc. for flower beds, trees and other structural items, we would move the sand to create a similar space to the one at home, though not as large of course. It meant we could stand and look at it, get an overall sense, and have ideas about the spaces, the types of planting and the general structure. It was a surprise to us to find that it was the structure, features and sculptures that told much of the story of each garden, with the planting as backup. However, it is also true that many of the plants carry a meaning, or have a clear relationship with the particular garden they are in. Each garden area also has a particular herb that relates to its theme.

We had an interesting time finding local artists who would create sculptures expressing our ideas where the requirement outran our ability. It led to some good discussions. Catherine Walters, who helped us turn a school's flat drawing of a fair trade idea into a garden sculpture, also made the *Creative Energy* sculpture in the first garden area. Catherine described our garden as a living sculpture. When there are times that few people come, we tell ourselves that we are tending the sculpture.

During the year we owned Little Hayes but had not yet moved in, John spent time working at garden preparation. There were weed trees to be felled, rhododendron to be rooted out and a great deal of soil to be moved. We paid for some help, and did much ourselves. When the builders were working on the house, John lived in my sister's caravan and I would join him for a day or so midweek sometimes. There were times when the back garden looked like trench warfare, and an alarming moment when I came round a corner of the house and saw the small digger, borrowed from the builder, lying on its side and no sign of John! Fortunately he was fine, just seeking help to restore the digger to the upright position.

No one had cared for the garden for some years and the boundary laurel hedge arched some fifteen feet each way from its rooted position, and this is just one example of what we were dealing with. To restore the vegetable garden, John put on all his tree-climbing protective gear, and went in with a strimmer among extremely high, thick nettles and other weeds, before he could get anywhere near the possibility of seeing and digging the earth. Reclaiming the white peach tree in the greenhouse carried other challenges; it had been so neglected, but great was our excitement when the love and care we expended meant we were picking sun-warmed peaches to eat. We concentrated on the garden areas one by one, and as they took shape and grew there was equal pleasure.

Shortly after we moved in it became clear that we needed more help. All the work at that time was beyond my strength and there were obvious times when two people, at least, would make the work much easier. John found the GrowWell project, which is a gardening project for people with mental health problems. They brought skill, strength and energy and our progress in establishing the gardens would have been very much slower without them. The people who came with the project found the quiet, privacy and peace of the gardens helpful. It was a partnership of great mutual value that we still benefit from.

People often ask us where we get our ideas from. The inspiration for the garden areas, or gardens as we often say, despite it all being in our one garden, came from the Ignatian Spiritual Exercises. Ignatius is a saint of the 16th century. As a young man he fought in the Siege of Pamplona and was seriously wounded. During a long convalescence he read the Bible, the lives of the saints and stories of knights. He was so inspired by the lives of the saints and the Bible that he became a monk, and in time founded the Jesuit Order. He became puzzled by the way so many good Christians made bad decisions, and so developed what is known as the Spiritual Exercises.

His suggestion was that when a serious decision had to be made you should take thirty days of prayer to consider it. Each day the retreatant speaks to a spiritual director, who sets the Bible passages to pray with that day. The first days are about knowing God's love for you, and where you are in reality with that. This is followed by four 'weeks': knowing yourself as a loved and forgiven sinner; discipleship and the life of Christ; the Passion of Christ; and then the Resurrection, which ends with meditations on finding God in all things. During these many days of prayer the aim is to know God's will for you in the decision you have to make. Our gardens follow the pattern of the Spiritual Exercises, so the ideas came from them, and it was like interpreting one language into another. How to express the Spiritual Exercises in plants, structure and features became the subject of our discussions over the next five years.

We had long theological debates, for there is nothing like interpretation to push you into thinking about what is really meant and how we understand a particular part of Christianity now. How do we express God's love?, for example: tricky enough in language to say what you mean, let alone in a garden. We were very clear that we wanted to avoid the sentimental views of this and include the gritty side of love, like loving enough to let go and to allow the ones you love to be free to make good and bad decisions for themselves. It helped that we had each done the Spiritual Exercises at different times, and that I had trained to take people through them. Not that we had a consecutive thirty days to spare, but there is a way of doing the exercises in daily life which takes about a year to eighteen months which we had followed. We had both found the experience very helpful, leading to many more insights than just particular decisions. We found it very helpful that Ignatius sees honour or dishonour, health or sickness, wealth or poverty as unimportant, the most important thing being that you are following God's will. Creating these gardens and making reflective space available was our interpretation of God's will for us, and our willing response. It has also been a great gift to us, pushed us to grow and think about what we really mean in our faith, and fulfilled the dream that began for us so long ago. As you can see from the comments at the end of the book, those who come find a gift here too.

It is my hope that whether you visit the gardens or not, the imaginative journey and the ideas about both faith and the environment will inspire thoughts for your own spiritual journey.

The journey round the gardens

Welcome to our gardens. We have created a reflective mini-pilgrimage round our garden with five garden areas that, in synergy with environmental issues, follow the Christian spiritual journey. They follow the pattern of the Ignatian Exercises, but if that doesn't mean anything to you, that will not affect your experience; it seems to be a template that reflects most spiritual journeys. The Ignatian Exercises are a pattern of imaginative meditative prayers, based on Bible passages, that are followed in the company of a spiritual director. They were designed by St Ignatius Loyola to help Christians make good life decisions. There are further explanations as this becomes relevant to the journey.

After describing each garden area, I explore the environmental issues that are related to the particular garden, and then the spiritual, theological thinking that is relevant to that part of the journey.

So here, in imagination, we start by taking you through the campsite beside us, and through the 'secret garden'-style of door at the very back of the garden ...

The Garden of the Loving Creator

The first area of the garden is about knowing the love of God, the Loving Creator, the Source, whatever name you would use for that otherness that Christians call God. Ignatius begins his Spiritual Exercises with a 'Principle and Foundation' (seems a good place to start!) that he sums up as 'knowing ourselves loved by our Creator'. In 21st-century Christianity we frequently talk about the 'love of God as Father' and about being 'loved by Jesus'. Knowing God as our Creator feels different – though a normal view in the Hebrew Bible (Old Testament), where the writer of Psalm 139 talks of there being no place where God is not, and of God forming us in our mother's womb.

Perhaps the discoveries of science have made Christians reticent about talking about God as our Creator. It is worth exploring the difference it makes when you bring this view to the front of your thinking.

So standing inside the entrance gate, on a semi-circular patio, looking down into the Garden of the Loving Creator, you are invited to join me in exploring some of its content and ideas.

Down one side of this area is a yew hedge. Yew can live for 2000-3000 years. No one is quite sure though, as yew trees have the capacity to split when branches are heavy, without succumbing to disease. They also produce shoots from old wood. The longevity led to the tree being connected with eternity, resurrection, and it was common on holy sites long before Christianity. Yew trees are very poisonous, so they are possibly also on holy sites to keep animals away from the graveyard. You will find older churchyards have a yew tree near one of the doors. Yew trees also offer healing. Two drugs used in chemotherapy, taxol and taxotere, were originally made from yew clippings to heal some breast cancers. These drugs, now made synthetically, have also been effective in treating some other cancers.[1]

The garden's path is made of slate chippings. This is because slate has been through most geological processes, melting, pressure, etc. and is generally formed from older rocks. On one side are cordylines and a cabbage tree. They look exotic and as if bursting from the ground. Sometimes in summer they flower, one long, unusual-looking bloom. We wanted something that indicated creation was not all pretty and sweet, but unruly, unexpected.

The other side of the path has a twisted hazel tree. Every twisted hazel comes from one branch of one tree where the DNA went funny. Hazel can only be reproduced by propagation, not by planting any of the nuts. The beautiful twisted stems are valued by flower arrangers. We all have unique DNA and part of it will contain the potential for the illnesses, the quirky bits in our particular body. We claim here the bits we don't like as well as those we do.

DNA

In my DNA
a unique twist
on family patterns.
So just me.

In this DNA
the illness
and the talent
twist together
in holy harmony,
sung in me.

A little further down the path there are wild daffodils in early spring, followed by bluebells in late spring. At first we tried to dig the bulbs out to move them elsewhere. Then we discovered that bluebells and daffodils have been around for millions of years, and so were rightfully in the creation garden. We also have there some of the nine Anglo-Saxon sacred herbs for healing. In today's English these are crab apple, mugwort, plantain, watercress, chamomile, nettle, chervil, fennel, atterlothe. (There are various spellings of this last one, and despite some guesses, no one is certain which herb this is.) Healing of body, mind and spirit is something we all need as part of our life's journey. About a third of the stories we have of Jesus in the gospels are about healing. So in this part of the Garden of the Loving Creator we just want to underline that healing is a natural part of creation; what we need for healing is there in creation to be discovered.

On the other side of the path, under the cabbage tree, is a small statue of a mother with child. Birthing is so much a part of creation that we wanted to represent it in some way. There is also the link, for those who see it, with Mary and Jesus.

There is a small oak tree on the corner of the path which sometimes has tiny 'oak apples'. Some of these may be smooth, others like a little fir cone. These are one of nature's examples of genetic modification. Gall wasp larvae change the DNA of the bud so that it grows into an 'apple' instead of a leaf. As bugs, they eat the soft inside of their round birthplace and then burrow their way out.

You then come to a sculpture called *Creative Energy*. Dancing at the top of the structure, and forming the sides, are many small human figures, each made from a waste plastic bag bound with rubbish cable. Joined at foot and hand, the figures create hexagons. Hexagons are the shape of a 'benzene ring' of carbon atoms, part of the molecule of many organic substances and a building block of creation. Catherine Walters, a local artist, was commissioned by us to make the sculpture, and was so interested in the idea that she went on to create other sculptures based on different chemical formulas.

The Garden of the Loving Creator 23

As you round the corner you come to the part of this garden we think of as 'loving enough to let go'. As any parent of teenagers will tell you, letting go is hard, and needs a lot of love and wisdom. God does not control us, we are not puppets on strings, but free to make our own choices for good or bad, free to make mistakes. God truly loves us with that unconditional love which leaves us able to grow.

Here we have a lush area of ferns, with another sculpture, a sphere held by two hands. If you look closely you will see that one hand is female and one male, and the position is such that the hands are just about to let go. A small fountain flows from the top. I think of this sculpture as God letting go of the world; such a risk, such a depth of love. Nearby, in the spring, you will see bleeding heart plants. Catholics who visit the garden tell me that the bleeding heart of Jesus image is connected to this plant. Later in the summer there are plants called love-lies-bleeding. Letting go is not without cost.

The small maze at the end of this garden is there to help you think about how you feel loved by God today. In the Ignatian Exercises you do not go further in the journey until you are aware, within, of the deep love of God. To honour this insight of the Exercises, we have created a space with flowers, broken pots, stones, thistle-type plants, and the inevitable empty spaces that come with having plants for different seasons. At the entrance to the maze is a pile of stones; we invite people to take one and to put it where they feel they are with God today, from in the middle of the maze to off the edge.

In the centre of the maze is a young ginkgo biloba tree. This species was found in an isolated valley in China, a remnant of the earliest form of tree which was present throughout the world before the Ice Age, and is found in fossils dating back 270 million years. The tree offers food, wood and healing, and has long been used in traditional medicine: God knows our needs and provides for us. There is a bench in the maze for you to sit and rest and to look back over this garden area and reflect on the love of the Creator.

Creation

From the beginning of time
all of creation is there.
From Adam to now a line
God gifted into our care.

```
                    So said Science once,
                    faith a given stance,
                    Genesis its source.

                    It is no longer so.

     Chaos                                    Butterfly wings
                                           a storm
          myths of beginnings
                         random
     possibilities                    beak upon beak, develops
                              and claw
             God      Wisdom
          black holes            and fossils, so so old
     millions, billions of years       eons of time
          Science               discovery        changes unending
                         Faith sees God in all
                              All is holy.
```

The environmental idea in the Garden of the Loving Creator

Each of the garden areas has an environmental theme in synergy with the Christian spiritual journey, and the theological ideas within it. For this garden the particular environmental issue is renewable energy; energy that provides electricity, but is not derived from finite fossil fuels, which we now know damage the planet. Instead electricity can be made from renewable energy, from wind, wave, biofuel or sun – new technologies that we still have much to learn about. So there is a structure adjacent to the Anglo-Saxon herbs for healing which demonstrates how we can make power from waves. There is a paddle at the front which can be moved slowly backwards and forwards to create a wave. Green floats move up and down with the wave. This operates the pedal of a bicycle, turning the back wheel with a small dynamo, and quite quickly you see the rear light of the bicycle light up. Water has its own weight and power; there is a technique when working the structure whereby you 'feel' the movement of the water and know the right moment to add the swish of the paddle.

As you leave this garden you pass the solar fountain, another example of renewable energy. If there is even bright cloud you should see a little water flowing from the fountainhead in the middle of the solar panel. In bright sunshine there is a good flow of water, and many people have lots of fun being a cloud by shading the panel with their hands and then taking them away. We have had some bother keeping this feature working however, more to do with having a pump that can cope with variable electricity, and the occasions when the water in the tank runs out because the fountain has been too vigorous, than with the solar panel itself. New technologies take some work and trial and error. However the 4 kW solar panels that we have on the garage roof make half of our daytime electricity needs in an average year, without any of the same kind of bother as we have with the garden feature.

On June 7, 2017 the National Grid reported that, for the first time, renewable energy had supplied more than half of the UK's needs for that day. Gentle energy, I call it, one that means the footprint we leave on earth is smaller and more sustainable. However, like with all new technologies, there has been plenty of opposition and resistance, both from individuals and powerful companies. The UK has a considerable opportunity for wave power, both the barrage kind at estuaries and the kind using the power of the sea. However there has been little government funding for its research, though the Scottish Executive is funding wave farms using tidal energy in several places, and they have challenged the UK government to follow suit. If you look at the possibilities for the River Severn estuary you learn something of the struggles with these new technologies.[2] The 10-mile version of the plan for the Severn estuary is estimated to be able to supply 5% of the UK's electricity needs. The barrage installation would last twice as long as a nuclear power station for less cost, and with no radioactive residue to deal with and greater energy security. It looks like a win-win situation, until you learn of the competing environmental needs of the birds who use the mud flats and the unknown possibilities of flooding further up the River Severn at times of high rainfall, each issue with its own group of campaigners. Projects have been proposed since as early as 1849 and still nothing is resolved.

Human beings are resistant to change, particularly if it could affect them. The resistance to a wind farm near where I live in Cannock Wood, Staffordshire, prevented one being built, and that is echoed in many places. Financial encouragement, however, prompted many to 'invest' in photovoltaic solar panels that turn light into electricity. We were one of the first in the West Midlands to have a 4kW set of solar panels installed on our garage roof in 2003. We thought it was worth the risk then in order to help establish the technology. Solar panels were significantly more expensive then, and with less of a tariff benefit than later installations. Although there was some government help with the overall cost, it will take the life of the solar panels for us to regain our financial costs. In Germany, however, the operator of a photovoltaic system is guaranteed a feed-in tariff for each kilowatt-hour fed into the electricity system for twenty years. Germany has more wind and solar energy than any other European country, and private citizens and farmers own almost half of the renewable energy projects.[3]

Human beings also have great innovative capacity and can find ways round most difficulties. For example, there are now more wind farms out at sea than was first thought possible. The consequences of climate change require us to be far more enthusiastic and creative about finding gentle ways to live on earth. The demand for electricity, and all its conveniences, increases, and will increase more as electric cars become the norm. Are we willing to focus on the research that renewable electricity needs; to accept these changes in the landscape; to love the world enough to look beyond our own needs to those of future generations and of the planet itself?

The thinking behind the Garden of the Loving Creator

It is important to be clear here that I accept and enjoy the findings of science about the universe, the planets and the world we live in. I particularly like the way new discoveries have added a few billions of years or so to the age of the universe. The theory of evolution makes sense as far as I can understand it. In scientific terms a theory holds force until disproved; with the theory of evolution so far, instead of being disproved, it has been upheld by many continuing discoveries.

So I find it puzzling when people of faith cling to the myth stories of the beginning of creation in Genesis as though they are scientific truth and historically, literally true. If such were the case you would immediately be faced with which of the two accounts of creation in the Book of Genesis is the one you see as 'true'. The one in chapter 1 where God creates light, water, land, plants, fish, birds and animals, and then a man and woman in the image of God with the commission to serve and care for creation? Or the one in chapter 2 where God creates a man from the dust of the ground first, then God plants a garden, forms animals and birds for the man to name, and lastly, as these were not sufficiently satisfactory companions for the man, God makes a woman from the rib of the man? They cannot both be literally and historically true. Clearly there is a different kind of truth in operation here.

Myths, and origin myths in particular, carry deep truths about the relationships between human beings, between human beings and God, and between human beings and their culture. In their telling of how we are here, they explore why we are here and how we are responding to the gift of life. These are not scientific questions, though I find the 'how' of the unfolding of the universe a matter for great wonder and delight. Most cultures have an origin myth; the Genesis myths assume that God is the initiator of the universe and remains in relationship with it. That is something I can identify with. An insight from them I particularly like is that we are both dust and the image of God.[4]

In the work I do as a spiritual companion (spiritual director) I have been greatly inspired by the Spiritual Exercises of St Ignatius of Loyola. The aim of the Exercises is to bring people closer to knowing the will of God for them, and to grow in the love of God. The very beginning, called the Foundation, is set out for the pilgrim to explore the love of God, and their love for God. When I did the Exercises myself this took a considerable time where I looked back over my life in prayerful conjunction with set scripture passages. In the original text of the Exercises it does not look like a long series of meditations, but who knows? Ignatius was clear that the spiritual director should fit the meditations to the directee. It is an important stage, awareness of God's love, because the reality of your relationship with God underlies all the stages of the Exercises.[5]

How do you know that God loves you? Those I listen to talk of a presence in their lives that is loving, encouraging, compassionate. Those who don't experience this kind of feeling refer to scripture, the story of Jesus and the doctrine of the church that tells of God's love for us. However, I find that for most of us the image we have of God is not that clear and consistent. We might say that God is love, but our responses and actions often reveal images that are very unloving. Our first experience of God is through our parents, but these are flawed human beings and with the best will in the world cannot give that perfect, unconditional love that God offers. The journey of separating god mum and god dad from God who is God, is a considerable part of the adult spiritual journey.

The judge, the schoolmaster, the policeman, the controller

are among other images that appear regularly when people talk about God. There are also the many things that take the place of God, recognisable in that they hold greater importance in our decision-making. Things like money, sport, holidays, clothes, cars and various other possessions, in reality can hold a greater place in our life than God, despite what we might tell ourselves. It is an interesting spiritual exercise to look at your bank account and how you spend your money, or to assess how you spend your time; not to do this in any judgemental way, but simply as a reality check. Most of us have a split between the image of God that we know in our heads, and the one that lives in our guts. Wholeness is the invitation to bring these together in the light and love of God.

My earliest memory of sensing the presence of God is when I was about four years old and hiding behind a long curtain, whilst my parents and other family members were enjoying the first fresh pineapple they had had, some years after the Second World War. One wealthier aunt had brought one that Christmas. I was momentarily aware of a great love, which I put into words by sticking my head through the curtains and saying, 'Oh the Holy, Holy, Holy Ghost.' Of course the adults laughed, not in an unkindly way, but for me they were the only words I could find to belong with the feeling.

Growing up in a Christian family I learned from my parents, and at church, of God's great love for us so that Jesus came to save us and be with us. As an adult I was compelled to recognise that what I said did not match the deeper feelings I had. Through prayer counselling I was enabled to own that Jesus was the only person of the Trinity I related to. Despite that early experience, a ghost, however holy, was scary to me, and the experience of growing up after the war in the bombed and devastated area of the East End of London, near the docks, had left a deep image of God the Father as one who either threw bombs or was helpless against them. Who would want to pray or draw near to such a god? Similarly with other images, the controller, the headmaster – better to keep a low profile than to try to draw closer!

To accept, deep within, that God loves unconditionally and truly is a fundamental part of the Christian journey; a freeing one, I believe, that also means other characteristics of God unravel and reweave in a more wholesome way. Just as one example: If a long-held belief, or hidden feeling, is that God controls the world, understanding that God is Love opens up many questions. If God is controlling the world, then why is it such a mess of violence and disasters? But how can Love control? Love is not love if it forces, *makes* the beloved behave or act in particular ways. The risk of free will is that people make wrong choices, disastrous choices, but it is Love's way to give us that freedom, and to still love and be beside us when we do make mistakes.

The Loving Creator invites us to consider that unselfish love that is a reflection of the Creator. St John writes 'God is love, and those who live in love live in God and God lives in them' (1 Jn 4:16). It is a common passage for weddings, but this kind of love is not easy. When Jesus says 'love your neighbour as you love yourself' he is not promoting an easy, soft option for life. The kind of compassion the Good Samaritan shows in the passage where Jesus illustrates this law carries risk and expense. It also crosses the tribal, racial divides that cause so much of human violence. Having or receiving compassion that recognises our common humanity, rather than the labels that divide us, takes us into both the front lines of conflict and the depths of love and care.

So the invitation of this first part of the pilgrimage is to recognise the way we actually do love, and the kind of love we recognise in God. This is to accept where we really are when it comes to love, so that we can see where growth is possible.

In gratitude

For the gift of life,
to appreciate beauty,
to feel the sun, smell the rain,
watch the trees respond to the wind,
great gratitude to God.

For the gift of life,
to explore possibilities,
test my strength and abilities,
learn and grow, respond to ideas,
great gratitude to God.

For the gift of love,
knowing another,
part of a family,
for companions, friendship, fun,
great gratitude to God.

The Garden of the Loved and Forgiven Sinner

The Ignatian idea is that you cannot recognise that you have sinned until you know and experience God's love. So in this garden the invitation is to face up to the things we do wrong, and in God's love, to know the forgiveness that frees us to grow and move on.

When you approach this garden area you immediately see a rubbish tip. In our minds it is like a beach, where rubbish has washed up on the shore. The first set of rubbish there did indeed come from a beach in Cornwall, where we even found black plastic bin liners to put the rubbish in. Most of the rubbish on our 'beach' now comes from the edges of Cannock Chase, a beautiful area of countryside where, unfortunately, people also dump rubbish. So there is a yellow car bumper and plastic bottles; a broken microwave from our house; a builder's protective hat from the beach, and various other items.

Some people are shocked to see rubbish there; but on the other side of the path, not quite so obvious, are three leaf bins where we collect fallen leaves from the garden to make leaf mould. We can destroy creation, or we can cooperate with creation. It is our choice. So the rubbish shows the mess we can make of the gift of creation. The leaf bins show what nature does with its waste. The advantage of making leaf mould is that we do not need to use peat. Leaf mould, made by layers of leaves with thin layers of soil and a scattering of lime squashed down and left, is as acid as peat and as friable for the soil, but it takes only three to four years to make. Peat takes thousands of years to form, has its own unique habitat and is a good CO_2 sink. However, it can be used to destroy creation. The practice of burning peat releases old CO_2 into the atmosphere.

A study by universities from the UK, Germany and Indonesia calculated that, in addition to creating the immediate hazards for human safety and health, the fires of 1997 in Indonesia released 0.81-2.57 gigatonnes of CO_2 into the atmosphere. This was the largest increase in atmospheric carbon since records began in 1957.[6] Farmers in Indonesia had long practised burning small areas of forest to increase their land, however larger farms, companies and government clearing wider areas, plus the dryness of the El Niño season, led to managed fires getting out of control and reaching into deeper layers of peat.[7] Unearthed, an award-winning Greenpeace journalism project, reported in 2017 that forest fires are now the new norm for Indonesia, and that the forest fire emissions of CO_2 there in 2015 equalled the annual CO_2 emissions of the UK. Due to climate change, we are now seeing more wildfires on larger scales than previously known. This affects all life, plant, animal and human, and also increases the CO_2 in the atmosphere.

Ahead in this garden, is a sculpture made by students at Stafford Art College. It is a set of screens made to look like bar codes, fixed individually on a zigzag path. The students knew, as we did not, that a shop-till scanner recognises bar codes by three pairs of thin lines, the beginning, middle and end of the bar code, denoting 666, which is the number of the beast in the Book of Revelation (13:18), though this connection was not the intention of the inventor of the bar code.[8] It interested me that this part of the Bible was known to some of the students, whereas we had to talk about our other ideas in environmental terms to them, as only one of them knew the Christian values we were intending to represent. The raw rubbish at the beginning is followed by screens on greed, anger, brokenness. The winding course of the screens symbolises that it is confusing to change and to try to live in a different way. As you move through the screens the theme changes to that of reworking and reweaving, until, on the last one, rubbish cable is used to form a vine with flowers made from plastic rubbish. Over the years groups have updated the screens, as the weather has corroded or damaged the originals. I have noticed that the plastic breaks down much more quickly now, possibly indicating a shift in the type of plastic used.

The path through the screens is made of wood bark, a reused product of forestry, and it leads to a straight path, representing the 'straight and narrow way', a reference to Jesus' words about the difficulty of the way to the kingdom (Mt 7:13–14, KJV). In the past, when pilgrims visited a shrine to express penitence, or to pray for healing, they would walk barefoot over stones, some even went on their knees. So this path is made of cobbles, with a straight flowerbed beside it. There we grow sage, for wisdom, and thyme, because it takes time to change. We also try to grow honesty, as you need to be honest with yourself to change, but we have a losing struggle with slugs and snails. There is always honesty at some point of the year, but it is gone usually by August and has never established itself. We are hoping to find a different space for this. Pansies, for thoughtfulness, have the same experience. In the late spring and early summer there is wild garlic, traditionally seen as protection against evil, and a plant called Jacob's ladder to represent struggle. Both of these grow well.

Next to the path runs a rubbish 'stream': water being represented by plastic bottles and any pieces of blue plastic we can find. The rubbish is a symbol for all the sins we commit. This 'stream' runs under a little bridge on the path, at the point where the path turns in a semicircle. In the middle of the semicircle is a fountain with real water coming in a spout from three different-sized rocks. Ignatius encourages our sorrow over and resistance to any deed or thought that is wrong.

Repentance means 'to turn, to change your direction', so the path then turns, and the rubbish 'stream' becomes a fountain of living (flowing) water. This shows what Jesus offers to those who

are sorry and want to change, so that, in the healing nature of God's mercy, the rubbish in our lives can become like life-giving water. Soapwort (*saponaria ocymoides*) is planted beside the rock fountain; soapwort's leaves can be used for washing, and are particularly good for cleaning old tapestries without damage to the threads and fabric.

As you complete the turn, you face a round gazebo with a table and chair inside and a hexagon-shaped stepping stone in front of it. Hexagons are a significant shape in our gardens: if you find one it means we are wanting to underline the spiritual importance of the idea there. The whole gazebo was originally intended to be a hexagon shape, but the drawing given to Mike, the friend who made it for us, was indistinct. After someone has worked iron to make a beautiful round shape you do not return it and say you wanted a different one! The round shape actually looks more including somehow, and the whole thing sits on a hexagonal base. The idea is that it is a place of welcome, now you have 'turned round', a kind of homecoming, just as Jesus illustrates the way God welcomes us in his story of the prodigal son (Lk 15). At the base of the fountain there is a dry water feature, a continuation of the 'stream' but this time made of waste blue plastic balls. Strong winds often mean we find them in unusual places, but the use of water in gardens has environmental consequences (loss of water and the energy required to move it) and we wanted to demonstrate other possibilities instead of real water features.

The hedging round the garden here is mixed, because people are all different. There are stepping stones leading across a small lawn to the bowl of a font with a tiny fountain bubbling up inside it. When we thought of having a font here we approached the then Bishop of Wolverhampton, Rt Rev Mike Bourke, who was the patron of the gardens then. Mike put us in touch with the Bishop of Birmingham, who had had to close a church and make it redundant, and we were offered the font from this church, if we would fetch it, and would promise to return it to the Bishop of Lichfield if the nature of the gardens changed. We also promised that it would not be a birdbath, so a 'wellspring' in the font fitted that requirement as well as the theology we wanted to express. It took four men to carry just the bowl from a lorry across the garden. Being in the garden has given a new and different life to the font, which is just what the decision to follow Jesus, expressed in baptism (Christening), is meant to offer us. Whether the promises are made for us, as when a child is baptised, or whether we make them ourselves, baptism is an outward expression of a desire to be part of the Christian family.

We try to have white flowers by the font, and have established a pretty white cyclamen. The lilies of the valley have mostly moved themselves to the raspberry bed; snowdrops came for a while, then disappeared; white busy Lizzies are swiftly eaten by slugs and snails; but a Madonna lily has survived well for some years now. There is a dove pattern in the pathway here, recalling the baptism of Jesus, and the presence of the Holy Spirit at baptism. This pathway leads to the next garden area, on discipleship.

The environmental idea in the Garden of the Loved and Forgiven Sinner

Every civilisation has to deal with its waste; dumping, burning, burying, using rivers and the sea, these are all ways by which we have dealt with the difficulties of rubbish down the centuries. Yet never has there been such a throwaway society as ours. Today, in the developed world, mountains of clothes are thrown out after very little wear; there is an expectation of continually upgraded models of electronic devices; food is thrown away uneaten; and then there is plastic. This material is not yet 100 years old but is now forming islands of waste in the oceans and microscopic particles of plastic are increasingly present in our food chains. The increase in wealth and living standards has had a consequent increase in waste.

There have been some shaming statistics. Hugh Fearnley-Whittingstall hosted a series on television called *Hugh's War on Waste*.[9] In one programme he was pictured in a shopping centre standing on top of seven tonnes of clothes that had been thrown away. Hugh had ensured they would be recycled, but the shocking fact he uncovered was that in the UK we throw away this amount of clothing – every 10 minutes! Moreover, most of the clothes are thrown in a bin, not given to charity shops or recycling. This is very different from a practice a hundred years ago of 'turning a coat' to make it look new again. (For those who have not encountered this practice, you took the coat to pieces and restitched it with the outside material turned to the inside.)

My Nan wasted nothing when it came to food and would be horrified at the idea of a chicken being thrown away uneaten – let alone 9817 an hour just in the UK (86 million a year), according to Love Food Hate Waste![10] It is not just the chicken itself that is wasted, but the food produced for it, the labour, the transport and processing. *Hugh's War on Waste* revealed that in the UK a third of food purchased is thrown in the bin. To highlight this serious level of waste, Hugh memorably stood in a supermarket with a black rubbish bag, throwing a third of some shopper's goods directly into the bag to save them the trouble of having to take it home.

Raised environmental awareness has led to many initiatives to recycle, repair, reuse, and to find ways to save food from being wasted when it is still perfectly edible. One of the most creative is the rise of cafés and community stores which use the food that supermarkets would throw away, where people pay what they can. 'Wonky Veg' are now part of Morrisons vegetable range. There are websites offering recipes for leftovers, and sites like www.freecycle.org, so that no longer wanted goods can be reused. Humans are creative and once aware of a problem are good at looking for ways to solve it.

As part of our environmental commitment we have three compost heaps in the garden: one ready to use on the gardens, one to be left composting away, and the third to put the fresh garden and vegetable waste in. Composting is an old and well-tried method of reusing waste to make a valuable, natural garden fertiliser. There are books extolling the virtue of the compost heap, and different ways of activating them, but they are simply really just a basic way of dealing with garden waste. The natural soil where we live is poor woodland/glacial soil, but our vegetable garden has quality, fertile soil from years of compost being added to it. You can put nearly any garden waste on a compost heap, even thin hedge trimmings, it just depends how dedicated to it you want to be. Whatever you do, anything you compost does not then have to be transported, processed and dealt with by the local government waste department. It is well worth an untidy corner and a bit of labour.

We also collect and store rainwater from various roofs. We use it to flush the toilets and for the washing machine, and to water the garden, where that becomes necessary. The water used in gardens becomes an issue in the UK when we have a lack of rain in the summer. Hosepipe bans are one of the first responses of local authorities when there is a drought. We have a large garden and never water it all. I learned, when living in a Hertfordshire village, that country people do not water nearly as much as townies, but let the roots of plants go down to the water table in drier periods. We would never water grass, as it will always recover, but we do water annuals when they are first planted out, a variety of tubs, vegetables in prolonged periods without rain and in the greenhouses. We have 'food yards' (rather than 'food miles') when it comes to vegetables. We have hardly ever resorted to tap water for the garden in the twenty-four years we have been here, and there are usually only a couple of weeks in the year when we need mains water for the toilets. However, there are so many places in the world where people do not have safely treated water even for drinking and when we first decided to collect and use rainwater it was, and remains, in a measure of solidarity with people in that position. More than a billion people live without access to clean drinking water, still. Our experience certainly made us more aware of rainfall.

The plentiful supply of water means most people in the UK give little thought to wasting water unless we are in a drought situation. We are lucky in the UK. We have treated water of a high standard, which means that waterborne diseases of the past, like cholera, do not trouble us. We can drink tap water without fear, and we put this expensively treated water down the toilet without thought. We generally have plenty of rain. Water waste and water supply is a big environmental issue worldwide. In the UK we each use an average of 150 litres of water per day. However, this increases to an average of 3400 litres a day when the water that has been used in processing the food we eat and making the clothes we wear, etc. is added in. It takes over a million litres of water for just one person to have a nutritious, low-meat diet for a year. There is just not enough fresh, accessible water in the world for everyone to have the water needed for the Western lifestyle as we live it today.[11]

Water waste needs to be seriously addressed; we need to find ways to recycle and reuse it. There are people working on this. Singapore has addressed some of these issues, and has reduced per capita water use in the city by encouraging different practices. They have also developed what they call NEWater, which is high-grade, reclaimed water produced from used water. It passes through a variety of new techniques to make it safe to drink.[12] 'Waste not, want not' is a truer catchphrase than we realise.

In the early 1900s the quantity of waste of each household would have been considerably less than today. Food would not have been in packaging, but in paper bags, newspaper, or put directly into the shopping bag; the paper would be reused as firelighters or toilet paper. There would not have been the food waste because leftovers from one day would be incorporated into meals for the next. The increased standard of living most of us experience compared to then is great, but the levels of waste that have come in consequence are not good at all. Maybe we need to rethink the idea of enough.

What is enough? Do we have to be influenced by what our neighbours and family have, or by what we see on television? Is greater consumption making us content and happy? I am reminded of a story a Catholic priest told me after he had stayed in an area of Eritrea. There he met someone who was a tourist guide and learned he was the only one of his family who had a wage, and that his earnings served fourteen people. Visiting them the priest saw that the other family members were not sitting about doing nothing; they tended the animals, fetched water and grew vegetables. They all lived together with a very small space for sleeping, and they slept on the floor. Their kitchen was outside, and that was where their gathering space was also. It would look very poor in UK terms, but when I asked the priest if they were happier than people here in the UK, he didn't hesitate but grinned and said, 'Oh yes, much happier.'

Waste lament

Plastic, bottles, clothes and such,
mountains of the stuff,
chicken, cheeses, veg and grain,
milk just down the drain!

All just wasted, subjugated,
crushed, thrown, blown;
sea, land and sky
take the dirt, and the hurt.

I lament this way of life,
wish, pray, hope for change,
seek forgiveness, make amends.
Love, insight sends.

When I was a child, young and keen,
every time we left the beach my father said,
'Let's leave this place better than we found it,
we'll take some rubbish away.'
A model for today,
for the world, some would say.

The thinking behind the Garden of the Loved and Forgiven Sinner

One of the things that delights me about the Ignatian Exercises is that, before sin/wrongdoing is ever mentioned, you spend time learning to know that you are loved by God. It has often seemed to me that Western Christianity has emphasised sin at the expense of love, when it is so clearly the other way round in the gospels. Jesus forgives without hesitation, and sometimes without being asked, like with the man who could not walk and is let down through the roof on his bed by his friends (Mk 2:1–

12). Jesus engages with those who were regarded as sinners by their culture, and shows the interest and care that God has for them. To so many who are ill, he brings healing. Illness then was regarded as a consequence of sin, sometimes even a punishment for your sin, or that of your parents or grandparents. This ancient idea is harsh – it is bad enough being ill without receiving condemnation for it. However, there is a real truth that if you live in an unhealthy way it is not that surprising if you get ill. It is also true that illness can be caused by the community; much illness disappeared in Victorian times when drains were given proper attention. Illness can also be simply bad luck, a consequence of a particular genetic makeup in a particular environment, nothing to do with sin of course, either individual or communal.

Jesus also engages with those who misuse money. He goes to Zacchaeus, a tax collector, and accepts his hospitality. By the end of the meal and conversation Zacchaeus is generously giving money away (Lk 19:1–10). The Pharisees complain of Jesus spending time with tax collectors and sinners, but Jesus points out that those who are sick need a doctor. Jesus is angry with the 'good' people for their religious manipulation of rules and lack of true understanding. I remember a social worker telling me about a group of disturbed teenagers in a group session, talking about their fathers. One boy was speaking of his father's anger at some of his actions, and another said, 'You're lucky, at least your father cares about you enough to be angry, mine doesn't care what I do.' Of course there are fathers who are inappropriately angry and damage their children mentally and physically, I am not talking of that very clear wrong. It is more here that love cares what the beloved does, about what happens to them and how they are, and whether they are growing in the best way.

I am one of those Anglicans who was brought up on the Book of Common Prayer (BCP). One of the common phrases there is that we are 'miserable sinners'. This did not endear me to the BCP at all. However one time at Taizé, an ecumenical Christian community in France, I found I was singing 'Misericordias Domini', and looking at the English translation in their songbook discovered I was really singing of God's mercy. It occurred to me that the BCP was the first translation from Latin into English for worship, and that maybe to the people of that time the words 'miserable sinners' would inevitably connect with mercy, sinners under God's mercy. It enabled me to see the words in a different light and to focus more on the merciful heart of God. However penitent and sorry we are for the wrong we do, being a sinner knowing the merciful love of God is very different from being a 'miserable sinner'. I recall a Catholic friend telling of the joy of coming from confession, when God's love and forgiveness seemed so close. The BCP does also say in a variety of ways: turn from your wickedness and live.

Julian of Norwich, an early English mystic, says that 'sin is behovely', sin is necessary.[13] What can be necessary about sin? It may be inevitable because we are human and have choices about our actions, but necessary? I think so. When babies change from crawling to walking, they inevitably fall over, often at first, then less and less, until they are running about easily. Part of learning to walk happens through falling. As muscles get stronger so balance is attained. We are not God's puppets but children of God, if we choose that path, and that is just it: we have choice, all sorts of choices. It is inevitable that we will make wrong choices, and it is a necessary part of learning when we do. Wrong choices have consequences: we can damage relationships; increase in selfishness; hurt the environment; affect the community we are part of. To the deadly sins that are part of Christian teaching – anger, pride, envy, avarice, gluttony, lust and sloth – the enneagram adds fear and deceit. (The enneagram is an ancient tool for understanding yourself in relation to others.)[14] Each of these sins has complex variations, and there can be a right time to be angry or frightened, for example, but as an underlying attitude to life they have a deadly effect on the human spirit. If we focus on the sins, and there are times when they do need attention, it is easy to be caught by the miserable, wretched sinner message. If we focus on the Christian path where Jesus offers us life in all its fullness (Jn 10:10) and the command to love God, neighbour and ourselves, then the perspective is to grow in love. Then, in the attempt to grow in love, the recognition of sin will draw us closer to God and the searingly pure love God offers. This way – recognising that again we have eaten too much: gluttony; lost our temper or been aggressive and forceful: anger; thought that our way was best and insisted others follow it: pride; avoided opportunity: fear – these, and many other possible examples, can become a learning place to grow spiritually, and in the quality of the love we offer. To know that we are loved, loved and forgiven by Life's Creative Source, enables us to try again, to make amends if necessary, to say sorry, to grow a little more in unselfish love. It also draws us deeper into relationship with God.

Thaler and Sunstein, in their book *Nudge*, write of the brain having two systems: the automatic system, which is quick and instinctive, and the reflective system, which is slower and thoughtful.[15] We need both. I recall one Easter long ago, I had carried the Easter candle into church, placed it in the holder and was singing the 'Easter Exultet' (a song of praise) when out of the corner of my eye I saw the candle begin to tip. Without thought my hand went out and caught it, still alight, before it could fall to the ground. The same automatic action comes into play when you face danger, from ducking a ball hurtling towards you to the quick reaction when a car comes unexpectedly round the corner. Fear too has its place in keeping us from danger. However if we are to change, learn from mistakes, find out new things, we need the reflective system. It seems to me that prayer encourages the reflective system that is part of our makeup, and encourages it towards the best of human endeavour. Prayer is so much more than the asking that so often seems to be the major component of prayer for many. The reflective waiting on God that comes with meditation and contemplation is the natural form of prayer for inner change.

There is an Ignatian practice called the Examen, or review of the day. In the presence of God you uncritically look back over the day that is ending. You reflect on what you are thankful for and what you regret. You notice where your mood changed and think about what happened before it; you notice where you have been destructive or unhelpful. You look for where God might have been involved, and basically reflect on the day that has passed and the day to come, then just be in God's presence.

To know that we are loved and forgiven when we do wrong does not mean that we don't care or can be casual about wrongdoing; it is an opportunity to grow towards the best we can be with God's help, if we choose to journey that way. Love received brings deep change within. It is part of the path of being a Christian disciple.

Divine grace

That you love the worst of me,
know the truth of me,
see my smallness
and my weakness,
and still love,
still offer love!

Thanks are too small for this.
I would hide from this,
such great brightness
in my darkness:
you're still there,
still waiting there.

And I will turn towards you,
ask for help from you,
accept a little love,
secret, healing love,
to bless my sin,
bring change within.

The Discipleship Garden

After knowing ourselves loved and forgiven, the next stage of the journey invites us to reflect on the life of Jesus, and to come to know him more closely. We are free to make the choice to follow him more fully as a disciple.

You enter the Discipleship Garden by following a path from the font, in which there is a stone representation of a dove, a symbol of the Holy Spirit. Ahead you can see a sculpture about fair trade: long poles in a sphere, each with fairly traded goods hanging from it, designed by children at St Michael's School, Lichfield. There is a supermarket trolley one side of it, and a child's ride-on red tractor on the other side. The supermarket trolley is attached by a chain to a telephone post that is conveniently near, as a reminder that the choices we make in a supermarket have global consequences. The red tractor symbol is used on produce to show that it is grown in the UK.

We grow raspberries and tayberries in rows in this part of the garden, since we hope that there will be good fruits from the discipline of being a disciple. In the middle of the path is a flowerbed with bedding plants and shrubs with yellow or blue flowers, the colours of the Mothers' Union logo. The Mothers' Union shows excellent discipleship worldwide in their work, particularly for poorer communities. Members of the Mothers' Union were very encouraging to us in the early years of creating the gardens. Groups came when the gardens were only partly done, supported us and made helpful suggestions. With one of their donations we bought the first plants for this flowerbed. Next to this bed are some blocks of stone and a narrow path: stumbling blocks and stepping stones, because in the journey of life difficult and hard things can happen to you that can become stumbling blocks to faith, or stepping stones to a deeper part of the faith journey. We have noticed that visitors relate easily to this kind of visual symbol.

The Discipleship Garden 55

This stage in the Ignatian Exercises follows Jesus' life. There are some key meditations in this stage about the choice to follow Christ; one is 'the Call of the King' where we imagine the call to service from a good earthly king, then move to considering the call from Jesus. Later is a meditation called 'the two standards'. Ignatius suggests we imagine the standards or flags of two sides in battle, representing the choice to be made between Jesus' Way and the attractions of the enemy; about the type of people we may become, and the loving responses we can make. This is a way of engaging the mind, will and heart in the choices that are part of being a disciple of Jesus. We do not attempt to represent these explicitly as you would encounter them in the course of the Exercises. However, we express the theme of choice (consumer choice) in the environmental issue of this area of the garden, and we made a variety of exits from this space.

One exit takes you to a wild area behind the Loved and Forgiven Sinners Garden, and the only way out is to go into that garden again. This is a representation of the wrong turns we sometimes make in our spiritual journey, the mistakes and wrongdoing. The gift from God is that we can always try again.

Another seeming exit between the lines of fruit is in fact a dead end. It is very pleasant when there are raspberries there to pick, but it doesn't lead anywhere. So many church groups that have come recognise the times in their corporate life when they have made a decision they thought was right for the church at the time but, although it gave some good fruit, it did not seem to really lead anywhere. This is also true for individuals.

A third exit is a gate through which there is a larger area of the Discipleship Garden, representing the idea of going deeper into the journey. You first encounter a play area, with a hexagon-shaped sandpit, some toys and a small slope that children always rush to and roll down. The idea of play surprises many visitors, but it is an important part of any spiritual journey. Beyond the play area is our representation of Lake Galilee, though many would see it as a garden pond! It has one beach side, and a clinker-built wooden boat opposite.

Getting such a boat when we are so far from the sea was a challenge. Fortunately for us we have friends in Sussex who regularly passed a farmer's field that had a number of old wooden boats in it, apparently abandoned, in long grass. Enquiry gave the information that they belonged to a father and son who used to regularly go fishing, but the son had tragically died and the father was no longer interested. The farmer was thinking of burning them. Pursuing this further, we ended up paying a small sum for one of the boats, and the father was delighted it would be used. The builder working on our house sent his brother with a long, flat-bed trailer to bring the boat up here. It caused some comment in a holdup on the motorway. An unplanned delight is that you can see the cross when you sit in the boat. In this area there are other hints of Jesus' life: a stream we have caused to run into the lake (living water), a set of bird feeders ('God counts every sparrow that falls', Mt 10:29), and a water jar fountain with red stones in the top (the wedding at Cana, Jn 2:1–11).

We grow borage as the particular herb for this garden, as it is meant to bring courage to the heart. Borage was traditionally placed in the stirrup cup of those setting out on crusade. We have recently added a bed of the Li Tim-Oi dahlia here, so called because of a competition to name a new dahlia reported on the BBC *Sunday* programme. Li Tim-Oi was the first woman to be ordained as a priest in the Anglican communion, in Hong Kong in 1944, and as it was the centenary of her birth, many of us who had worked for the ordination of women as priests in the Church of England wrote in for the dahlia to be named after her. Li Tim-Oi had the courage, humility and wisdom to follow a difficult path, and her life has been an inspiration to many women following in her footsteps.[16]

There are benches in this area to offer space for reflection and, with those at the side of the house, a chance to watch the reflections on the water. At the back of the house, a lovely suntrap, there is a circular labyrinth. We made this by stringing out the design, and with careful use of weed-killer over the string this gave us a labyrinth in three weeks. We went for the classical design where the one path to the centre goes in circles and appears to get further away from the centre, yet every step is taking you closer. Labyrinths are an ancient idea. Greeks, Egyptians and Romans made them long before Christianity came on the scene, but from medieval times they have been made in many Christian locations, notably cathedrals. There are suggestions that people used to walk them instead of undertaking the journey to Jerusalem, that they were used as a part of reflective prayer by pilgrims, and that clergy danced them at Easter.

58   *Through the gateways of a garden*

Also round the house are examples of some of the environmental choices that John and I have made. From here you can see the 4kW photovoltaic cells on the garage roof; the wood pellet central heating boiler; water tanks for collecting rainwater to flush the toilets and run the washing machine, and a hot tub, which also uses filtered rainwater and is heated by wood. It is possible to see our vegetable garden and greenhouse from here as well. We aim to grow organically, and have learned to pick what is ready to eat, rather than buy what we fancy and let garden food run to seed. People from different African cultures who have visited us tell us that they feel at home in the vegetable garden, as that is what they would naturally have in their own country.

Just by living in the West we all have a higher-than-world average carbon footprint. John and I are lucky enough to be able to undertake some large environmental decisions, our view being that it is an appropriate use of our 'more than enough' for living. Kathy Galloway of the Iona Community once gave a talk in Lichfield Cathedral where she showed how, even in the wealthy West, in general poorer people have a much smaller carbon footprint, though there is, of course, a big difference between those living with others and those living on their own. There are plenty of websites to give you ideas for action appropriate to your pocket. To measure your carbon footprint, visit www.carbonindependent.org

At some point it is time to return to the remaining exit from the first part of the Discipleship Garden. This gate leads to the Passion Garden, where the cross is central. There are some visitors who ignore both the Passion and Resurrection Gardens and go home from the reflection area, so I suppose that technically there is another exit too. It is easy to continue walking round the house to the gate and out onto the drive. Another choice people make as disciples is whether to sit lightly with the gospel or to engage fully with all that is offered.

Choices, choices in the supermarket,
so many types of crisps, of rice,
varieties of tea and cake and chocolate!
So many things I never thought of needing!
I only thought of feeding
family and friends.

Choices, choices in the paths ahead,
so many different ways to go,
excitement and adventure, how to know?
So many opportunities for living!
I simply thought surviving
was the only way you see.

Choices, Living God,
I am wondering what
Your choice would be for me?

Not painted in the sky
but written in my heart.
Help me know Your Way to be.

The environmental idea in the Discipleship Garden

When we first moved here all our heating was from oil, a fossil fuel coming from a long way away. We have no mains gas connection here, though we do have a Calor gas tank for the cooker. Gas is also a fossil fuel, though gas burns less CO_2 and has less environmental impact than other fossil fuels.

However, we wanted to be as carbon free as possible, and friends suggested a wood pellet bio-mass boiler as a solution. This burns pellets of wood, but wood of this era, so it is carbon neutral, unlike coal and oil. Carbon neutral, in this case, means that the amount of carbon dioxide produced in the burning process equals that absorbed by the tree when it grows. This means it is a continuing supply of renewable energy. Also, the pellets do not have to travel as far as oil does. They are made from waste of the wood industry and forestry thinning. To have a bio-mass boiler requires a large space to keep the pellets, and a place for the boiler, plus a little more regular attention than a conventional boiler. However, we were pleased to discover that the pellets are fed into the boiler automatically, which means it operates as any other boiler would. It was a learning curve to have one though. It is best to leave it running for a longer time than other boilers, and at a lower temperature, so that there is a more constant temperature.

The first year we had the pellet boiler the house seemed to be permanently cold, and I felt as though I needed a coat to go from room to room. While attending a local Green Fair we learned that it is best to have a buffer tank of water by the boiler, so the water coming through the system is at maximum temperature when the heating comes on. We found it a bit tricky to fit one in the highly insulated boiler house, but it meant the whole system worked well and we are glad we did it. On advice from the same friends, we kept the oil boiler and designed the system so that we could switch to it easily. It is rarely used, but it can take a week to ten days for the pellets to come when ordered so we are very glad of it then, and also on the occasions when the feed mechanism of the pellet boiler gets jammed and needs sorting.

Our next-door neighbours made a different choice when they started thinking about environmental issues and wanted to get off oil. They installed an air source heat pump. An air source heat pump works by taking some heat out from the outside air. Our neighbours installed under-floor heating pipes, which work best with this type of heat source. Our son, also with an air source heat pump, just has radiators that are generally 50% larger than the normal specification. Our neighbours firstly had the insulation in their house massively increased, to the extent that they moved out for six months to have it done, and are very pleased with the overall result. The whole system works like a reverse refrigerator and seems like magic to me.

Along with growing our own vegetables we have chosen to keep chickens, so for some things we have food yards rather than food miles. It does keep us very in touch with the seasons and seasonal food, and gives us tastier vegetables than we can buy. We find even shop organic carrots are not a patch on ours for taste, similarly with tomatoes, when we run out.

Food miles is a serious environmental issue, as all forms of transport cost the earth. We have friends who altered what their local supermarket stocked by informing them that they had formed a consumer group who planned to buy only fair trade or British food. You could name any food, and they could tell you how they could get it through one of those means. The one that comes to mind is the sticky toffee sauce that they persuaded the supermarket to source from the nearby Lake District, instead of Italy. Their actions altered the selection of goods in the local supermarket, showing the power of the consumer when we work together; the food miles saved meant that the fossil fuel used in lorries, ships and planes was significantly less. The group's work inspired the sculpture and red tractor next to the supermarket trolley in the first part of the Discipleship Garden.

The miles we travel personally is, of course, also a huge environmental issue. The highest cost to the environment comes from plane travel, where the fossil fuel emissions are 30,000 feet above us and so have a greater impact on climate change. Airplane travel has increased year on year and there are regularly contested plans to expand Heathrow, or build another London airport. Short journeys by air for business or pleasure are particularly damaging because planes burn fuel at a higher rate during take-off. Until we find a different fuel that is gentle on the earth it is worth looking for other ways to connect with people and to seek pleasure.

Some of my friends do not travel by plane at all. Some years ago, when we realised the environmental cost of air travel, we reduced to one excursion a year, of no more than four hours each way. I know there are those to whom this will seem a lot of travel, and those for whom it is very little.

We were then challenged (through our membership in the Iona Community) to further decrease our annual carbon footprint by 5%. The only way John and I can do this now is to reduce travel. We were stunned to find that if we changed to travelling by train to the south of Spain, instead of flying to Crete, just one year in three, we would each reduce our carbon footprint by 18%, so a 6% a year spread over the three years. It is more expensive, as train fuel is taxed whereas airplane fuel is not (no country charges tax on airplane fuel because of the competition between nations), but we will still enjoy a holiday abroad whilst leaving a gentler footprint on the earth. Recently we reduced this further to one plane holiday every other year.

For me it was a painful and costly decision as I love going to warmer countries with more sunshine than we have here. I remember thinking to myself, 'Has all this environmental stuff got to be costly and miserable?'

It is true that many of the mature environmental products offer a good return on investment, but we have been early users in some areas. So, as a compensation, we thought of getting a wood-burning hot tub, just for fun. Looking on the Internet we found one that is like a large half barrel, with one side sectioned off for the firebox and chimney. We filter rainwater into it, heat it with wood, and when we have finished, the water is filtered back into one of the rainwater storage tanks. It is labour-intensive, but brilliant fun. We tend to fill and heat the tub when grandchildren come to visit or we are feeling particularly in need of it. There is nothing quite like sitting in hot water, outside, when it is cold. We have even got out and rolled in snow and swiftly returned to the warmth. The grandchildren love it and so do we.

People make choices with environmental impact every day – especially those of us who live in the developed countries – from little choices about when to get up and what to wear today, to world-reaching ones like what we buy, where from, and how we travel. These choices express our values, desires and interests. They all have consequences for the earth.

The thinking behind the Discipleship Garden

The decision to follow Jesus, so to be a disciple, is a choice that happens gradually for some and at a special time for others, and Christian denominations have different ways of affirming this. I once heard a talk at Greenbelt (an annual Christian arts festival) that suggested that *just turning* in Jesus' direction, just starting the relationship, meant you were a disciple. This doesn't necessarily mean you remain a disciple, as people move in and out of faith all the time, but the exploration itself is discipleship. So in the Ignatian Exercises this part of the journey challenges your commitment as a disciple of Jesus and your relationship with him. It invites you to explore where you really are with Jesus.

The preparatory meditation is an imaginary call from an earthly king, linked to the call of Jesus. Later there is a meditative choice to be made between two standards or flags of the leaders, one the standard of Jesus and one of the enemy. It seems obvious, at first glance, that we would choose Jesus rather than evil, accepting the gospel virtues of compassion, forgiveness, seeing all as family, giving yourself for the sake of others; however the desire for wealth and goods, celebrity lifestyle and the 'me first' thinking pervading our culture can hook the best of intentions. So this choice is more about seeking your own clarity of judgement about where the hooks are that distract or turn you from a better way.

For the Ignatian meditations, discernment of God's will for you is an important part of the journey and there are a number of rules for discernment that Ignatius developed to help those giving the Exercises. The simplest one to share here involves ways of deciding between two choices of direction in life for yourself. Ignatius offers certain prayerful questions, like 'How would you advise a friend?'; and the suggestion to write out the pros and cons of each option, to look at them prayerfully; then to live for a week as though you have made one decision, then to do the same for the other option. It is very revealing.

Behind the meditations is the question: what lifestyle will you choose? Ignatius encourages us to use the life of Jesus as our benchmark. Being a disciple is not just a choice for Sundays, but one that affects every area of life. One of the challenges I sometimes give people, in sermons or Spiritual Direction, is to pray over their bank balance. There is nothing like the reality of where you spend your money to reveal your personal priorities. When I first did this exercise I was shocked to realise that we spent more as a family on petrol and the maintenance of cars than we gave away to charity. It took us a while, and serious conversation, to change this round.

It sometimes seems as though sex is the major discipleship issue for the church, not the use of wealth. The challenge to the Christian church is to redress that balance within its own concerns. Jesus says much more about our use of money than he does about sex. Behind the misuse of money and the preoccupations with sex and celebrity is often the, sometimes hidden, desire for power and control. Ignatius encourages indifference (in the sense of having no preference) towards wealth or poverty, honour or dishonour, health or sickness; these outcomes are not our priorities, the whole aim being to do God's will. The love relationship with God becomes our greatest desire and preoccupation.

Ignatius goes so far as to suggest that we should pray to attain spiritual poverty, actual poverty and society's insults so as to better imitate Jesus' experience. I sometimes wonder if the monastic virtue of poverty has prevented the discussion about the Christian use of wealth, the 'more than enough', from being more widely and fully explored. The great struggle in discipleship is to live by God's will and God's priorities rather than our own. It is to be so caught by the love relationship with God that our greater desire is to align our own will with that of God's, Jesus being the model and example that gives us insight and access into the heart of God.

In a village where I served as Rector I was told that 'those at church think they're all good and holy, but I can tell you they are not!' My response was that following Jesus was about *trying* to grow in good qualities, but that we all failed. Knowing the love of God meant that we could say sorry and try again. Those in the village who said this, sometimes meant goodness as in law-abiding and 'moral' behaviour, and there have been regimes that have used faith as a way of controlling populations to be moral and law-abiding. Following Jesus does not always mean being good in that sense though. God's priorities, as far as we can understand them, do not always fit that of a particular culture. The only law that Jesus gives in the gospel account is to love God, and to love your neighbour as you love yourself (Mk 12:30–31).

I have friends who are willing to break the law to challenge the possession of nuclear weapons and many other friends who regularly demonstrate against them. As disciples of Jesus they use the power of non-violence. You cannot love your neighbour and send a nuclear bomb over them. I am personally unconvinced by the 'just war' theories. War is barbaric and always evil. The most that can be said, in my view, is that it is sometimes the lesser of two evils. Many societal changes have happened because Christians have realised something is wrong. So slavery ended, employment laws changed, health care and education were offered to all. These changes were backed, and sometimes led, by a Christian understanding coming into focus and there are still issues we are working at – there always will be until we all live by Jesus' law of love.

Environmental issues underline this. For a long time we did

not realise that we were damaging the planet; we cannot take blame for what we did in ignorance. But now that we know things are wrong, it is very different. Care for God's creation, one way of expressing love for God, is part of discipleship. In Celtic thought God has two books: the big book of creation and the little book of the Bible. Columbanus, a monk of the sixth century, says 'those who wish to know the great deep, must first review the natural world ... Understand creation if you wish to know the Creator.'[17] Reverence for the natural world pervades the stories of the Celtic monks of that era. So Saint Cuthbert is accompanied by otters that dry his feet after he has been praying in the sea; Saint Kevin has a bird lay an egg in the palm of his hand, which he holds safe till it has hatched; and Saint Columba has a white horse who, when he recognises that Columba will soon die, lays his head against Columba's breast and cries. At the very least, these stories show a closeness to the natural world which few in our culture know. Finding ways of caring for the damage that has been done, along with ways to leave a smaller and gentler footprint, is a serious discipleship issue for today.

As members of the Iona Community one part of the Rule of life we follow is to work for peace and justice, and to care for the environment. This is seen as a natural outworking of following Jesus. Of course no one person can do everything. We need to discern our part and contribution to the general picture. We also need to love ourselves – love your neighbour as yourself, Jesus says. Play and space for reflection is as much a part of the life of a follower of Jesus as anything else. Jesus went to celebrations, enjoyed others' hospitality, and went alone to pray in the hills. It is hard to serve if you neglect yourself, and burnout helps no one. Sometimes it is worth asking what is actually behind your care for others if you do not adequately care for yourself.

So to choose to follow Jesus is to live as befits the values and priorities that Jesus teaches and lives. We continually need to discern with others how that works out with the knowledge and culture of the present day, growing in love as we do so. To choose any spiritual path inevitably involves choices of lifestyle and the direction your life will take.

I would follow you, brother Jesus,
live your will for me,
walk in your way,
discern the next step.

My will so often off this path,
wanting comfort now,
safety, wealth, health,
weaknesses to the fore.

Holy God,
you are welcome
in the secret places of my soul,
to effect the changes
only your love can bring.

The Passion Garden

The third exit from the Discipleship Garden, past the stumbling blocks and stepping stones, leads into the Passion Garden. When we seek to be disciples we inevitably encounter conflict within ourselves and with other people. Here, in the Passion Garden, we reflect on the Passion of Jesus – his conflict with the authorities of his day, and within himself, as he seeks to follow God's will. This circular garden is surrounded by a holly hedge, holly being connected with the Passion of Jesus through its blood-red berries and prickly leaves, and with his birth through the small white flowers which bloom in spring.

A large, full-size cross dominates this garden. It is a replica of the first one that was given to us by the builder who masterminded the alterations to our home. He and some of the children at the local church in Gentleshaw had made it for a church from old scaffolding planks, four making the upright, and four shorter ones the crossbeam. They had painted the cross black, with gold for where the body of the now risen Jesus had been. Every year, for a while, a group had carried the cross to the highest point around here, Castle Ring, an Iron Age hillfort, for a dawn service at Easter, and then, on round to the local church.

As with all things in church life, customs had changed and the church was no longer using it, so Roy, the builder, gave it to us. We repainted the cross fully black, as this garden is only about the crucifixion. It was then carefully placed on a spike that goes deep into the ground, and fixed centrally in this garden area. Over the years the wood rotted, birds nested in the hollow crosspiece and the cross needed replacing. However the replacement is exactly like the original – a dramatic and industrial-looking cross. Round the base is a circle of coal, with lumps that John was allowed to pick out from the stock of the last local supplier. Round the circle of coal is a pathway made of slag from an old iron foundry. This was a very industrial area with the coal mines a major employer, all gone and greened over now, but we wanted to honour the industrial past.

We place black pots, planted with red flowers, at the foot of the cross, and our aim is that all the plants in this area are red, in some way, at some point in the year. Sometimes people place something that is meaningful to them at the base of the cross: a glass heart, a toy car ... We generally leave these items for a year, unless the weather destroys them first. They are a symbol of someone's prayer. When I take a group round the garden, I always invite them to think about what symbols they would place round the cross to connect with the area they live in.

The slag path makes a crunchy noise when you walk on it. As you come to the mirror doors that are the exit from this garden, though, the path changes to become silent underfoot, because we are often hushed in the face of death. This surface is made from tiles of recycled car tyres, a material often used in children's playgrounds. We used mirror doors because as you approach death you cannot see what is ahead, only yourself and what is behind you.

Within this garden there is a meditation hut with two hexagon-shaped windows facing the cross; the hut is reminiscent of a Middle Eastern home at the time of Jesus; it is all too easy to forget that Jesus was a Jew. John built the hut out of breezeblocks and then a group of 35 Cub Scouts, suitably gloved, slapped render on by hand, as that was the method of building used in the Middle East. Their leader watched them for a while – then begged for a turn himself. The meditation hut is available for times of prolonged reflection.

By the hut is a tub with hyssop in it, and a cockspur thorn tree. A hyssop branch with a sponge of sour wine on its end was offered to Jesus when he was on the cross (Jn 19:29). Hyssop, grown widely in the Middle East, is a bitter herb whose flowers

and leaves are used for a variety of ills. The cockspur thorn is a variety of hawthorn that we bought for its particularly large thorns, about 2-3 centimetres long. We chose the tree to represent the crown of thorns that soldiers put on Jesus before he was crucified. One year, taking a group round shortly before Easter, I saw that the tree was about to burst into leaf. It made me very reflective on the state of the thorn bush the soldier used to make the crown of thorns. Certainly any leaves would have wilted very quickly, but it had not occurred to me that leaves could have been present on the crown.

On the other side of the tree is a space where we have 'grown' a crown of thorns, a thorny berberis. A short weeping Kilmarnock willow represents Jesus' hair, and is mostly surrounded by the berberis. Behind this, on a fence, we grow a passion flower climber. In my brother's house in London this creeping plant can take over a fence more than you would wish. Here, at about 900 feet above sea level, we are pushing our luck. If the winter is mild then it will still be alive in the spring, but mostly after one hard frost or another it dies. I grow a new one every year and keep it in the greenhouse over the winter. It fits this garden so well. The large layer of petals and sepals at the base, usually 10, are meant for the faithful apostles at the time of the Passion; the hair-like rays above the sepals represent the crown of thorns; the five stamens above them are for the wounds of Jesus; and the three pistils at the top for the nails.

Then you are by the exit from this garden, the quiet path of recycled tyres, and the mirror doors.

Suffering people trailing,
waiting - - -
for the test result,
the doctor's verdict,
food to eat,
war to end.

Suffering landscape, fading,
waiting - - -
for the rain to fall,
the sun to shine,
rubbish removed,
landmines cleared.

Suffering planet, heating,
waiting - - -
for laws to change,
action to be taken,
gentle footprints,
love for all life.

The environmental idea in the Passion Garden

The human suffering caused by climate change is incalculable, though charities like Christian Aid do their best to help alleviate it. The Lichfield diocese worked with Christian Aid, Operation Noah and the Riding Lights Theatre Company to produce a play highlighting the problem of climate change and to encourage action. There are some video excerpts of the play online with accompanying material to use in schools or small groups.[18]

One of the stories is about Bangladesh, where the per capita contribution to the world's CO_2 output is a fraction of that of the rest of the world, but people suffer disproportionately high consequences of climate change. The Deccan Delta flooded heavily in 2009 with cyclone Isla making a million people homeless. One consequence of Isla was that traditional farming became impossible. This is a continuing problem because of repeated flooding and rising tides and sea levels adding more salt to the land. Aid workers have helped in a variety of ways. Practical Action[19] has helped with floating gardens, a base of bamboo and water hyacinths. On this women have learned to grow vegetables for themselves and for market. Local people now build their houses on stilts to be above the floodwaters, and farm a variety of duck that copes better with salty water. Many people have now migrated to the big cities though.

We could think that this is a far-away, foreign problem, but Britain has recently suffered flooding from unusually heavy rainstorms. Tewksbury has been regularly flooded in recent years, leaving the abbey as an island a number of times, and the town suffered severely in 2012, as did a wide surrounding area, including flooding across the M5 motorway. London has a barrier on the Thames to protect Greater London from tidal and fluvial flooding, and the barrier has already been raised more often than was expected at its inception. However, in Britain we have the wealth to alleviate some of the suffering people experience. In the poorest areas of the world, millions suffer the worst impacts of climate change.

One of the consequences of climate change is that centuries-old farming techniques no longer work, as they depend on the knowledge of when to sow and harvest crops. The people of the Nsanje region of Malawi rely on rain-dependent farming practices. The Nsanje region is highly vulnerable to climate change, with frequent droughts and flooding which threaten food security. Christian Aid has been working with the people there for over twenty years, aiming to bring a greater resilience against the variability of the climate, and to raise people from subsistence level. They have worked with other agencies to establish approaches to water resource management that are rights-based, participatory and inclusive. Access points to water have been increased so that fewer households depend on one water pipe. The farmers have been learning climate-smart agricultural practices and irrigation methods, and have increased the diversity of the food they grow, which both helps with food security and gives more to sell. A recent drought, however, was so severe that it threatened all the work done in Nsanje.[20]

Raindrops are like liquid gold to farmers in the poorest countries of the world. Yet when the rains do come – and in many places they come erratically or with decreasing frequency – with no irrigation techniques available, most of that precious moisture is washed away, unused. Land is so dehydrated that people are unable to grow enough produce even to sustain their families; there seems to be no way out. So Practical Action has, with the help of communities, designed a simple hose-pipe drip system so that instead of parched, dusty fields, there are life-giving gardens brimming with hearty fruit and vegetables or sturdy columns of maize, year after year.[21]

Christian Aid has found that climate change is rendering traditional methods to tackle poverty inadequate. In Burkina Faso, for example, approximately 250,000 families rely on water from the Louda Dam, but as a result of changing weather patterns there has been insufficient water in it over the past few years. Christian Aid predicted in 2009 that, by 2020, climate change could leave up to 250 million more sub-Saharan Africans in poverty. It is unsurprising, in my view, that so many Africans risk the unsafe boats across the Mediterranean to reach greener and more prosperous Europe.[22]

Desmond Tutu said: 'Who can stop climate change? We can. You and you and you and me. And it is not just that we can stop it, we have a responsibility to do so that began in the genesis of humanity, when God commanded the earliest inhabitants of the Garden of Eden to "till it and keep it". To "keep" it; not to abuse it, not to make as much money as possible from it, not to destroy it.'[23]

During the early part of our time at the house we kept bees. A friend looked at where we live and said, 'You must keep bees here, it's ideal!' Well, I could write a lot about the steep learning curve, the different natures of the hives and the sheer delight of spinning honeycombs in a large drum, which splats the honey to the side of the drum where it runs down to the bottom and you tap it off in a jar. We kept bees for about fourteen years. In that time conditions for bees changed and they became much harder to look after.

Bees are important pollinators, and are seriously affected by climate change and agricultural practices. They semi-hibernate in the winter months, living in a slow crawl round the queen, keeping her warm in the middle, warming themselves there after being on the outside of the cluster. They feed the queen and themselves, but only a little while they are in this slow state. The warmer winters meant that they woke out of cluster too early for the pollen they needed, and the winters that have prolonged periods of snow interspersed with warmer weather are just as difficult for them.

Beekeepers can protect honeybees to a certain extent: treat them against diseases, add food to their supplies if necessary and generally look after them, but that is not the case for wild bees. In Europe bee diversity has seriously declined. In the UK three types of native bumblebees are now extinct, and six others are listed as endangered. There are similar declines in China and North America. A mix of weather changes, the use of some pesticides on crops (neonicotinoids are particularly bad for bees) and the destruction of forests has contributed to, or some would say caused, this decline. In China the decline has meant that people have to hand-pollinate some crops, like apples. As I well know, people are not nearly as good at this as bees. We have a peach tree in the greenhouse which flowers early because it is inside. We have a much better crop when I persuade an early bumblebee or two into the greenhouse than when John and I use a paintbrush to pollinate the flowers. 75% of our food depends on pollinators, and the honeybees cared for by beekeepers are not enough for this. Bees and other pollinators are very sensitive to changes in their environment and their decline is a good indication that our whole ecosystem needs its natural balance. Their suffering is a warning for humanity.[24] This is an example that shows creation itself is shouting at us humans that something is gravely wrong.

There is a sense in which the land itself suffers. It is not that land suffers as humans would understand it, but that human action destroys, damages and changes the fertility and natural state of the land. Nearby here there used to be a number of coal mines that, in this sense, caused suffering for the land as it was broken open, tunnelled and the coal mined. To do so, the fields and woodland were destroyed. It is natural that we have used the land as a resource, because of our own need to live, but I think a challenge to consider the needs of other species and the land itself is not out of place. Some farming friends I have talk of the land as 'a living entity'. They say that we should farm the land as though we will live forever, which means we should care for it to the very best of our ability, rather than use it just for today's needs and risk destroying it.

Where the coal mines have closed, the land has been restored to its natural beauty, but there are many homes around here that have a slope or tilt because of the tunnels beneath them. And

many in the past suffered and died mining the coal. As we
damage the land, we damage ourselves.

Your suffering, Jesus,
still touches people's hearts,
changes lives,
helps souls to grow.

Such an example
of being true to God's way,
keeping integrity,
accepting Love's path.
This is hard to follow;
only done with your
company.

The thinking behind the Passion Garden

Jesus' death on the cross is central to Christianity, so it is surprising how very many views there are about the meaning of the cross and the Passion of Jesus, and it is interesting how these ideas have developed and changed over the centuries. I share here the journey I am on with Jesus' Passion and how it holds meaning for me. This was behind our thinking as we designed this garden area.

As a child growing up in a vicarage the knowledge of Jesus' life and death was just part of normal living. I felt the sadness and horror of the cross especially in Holy Week, but also something of its power. When my Grandpa died, each of his grandchildren was given a small amount of money to spend in memory of him. I was very clear that I wanted a cross with Jesus on it over my bed, and not a dead Jesus but a risen one. I could not have articulated it then, but I recognise now that I somehow felt that the cross there was a protection against my very real fears of the dark. It was not that I stopped being frightened, nor that a piece of wood and metal had magic powers, but was a reminder of Jesus' love and power. I still have that cross over my bed, and since confirmation at twelve have worn a cross, again as a reminder of Jesus' love and power.

For a long time I accepted the view of many hymns, and some preachers during my teens, that the cross was about being saved from sin, my sin, humanity's sin. It is a very traditional view of the cross that our sins are forgiven by Jesus' sacrifice, that somehow we are 'put right' with God the Father by Jesus' death. Early Protestantism carried this further by seeing the wrath of God as requiring Jesus' death so that we can be put right with God. There are enough phrases in Paul's letters to seed this idea.

Early in my spiritual journey I had a poor view of God the Father where rage and wrath fitted well: one of those 'not gods' that the adult spiritual journey gradually reworks. As I grew to see Love as the major characteristic in every person of the Trinity, my views changed. When I thought of God the Mother seeing her son on the cross, it gave me a very different perspective. When I gaze at the cross, I see God there, with Jesus. Many Orthodox icons show symbols of the Father and the Holy Spirit with Jesus on the cross. I can see human sin, and the awful ways we can treat others when I look at Jesus on the cross, and I can also be convicted of my own sin, but I cannot see that God the Father needs Jesus' death to forgive us. It seems a dreadful thing to believe of a loving God. Walter Wink says that in the face of such a view the most religious response is to be an atheist.[25]

Jesus shows God readily forgiving when we are sorry, searching for us, calling us to love even enemies. Jesus goes round forgiving people their sins and healing them; some are healed just by this freely and intuitively given forgiveness. The

Scribes are shocked by this, in their view that only God forgives sin (Mk 2:1–12). Peter struggles with the idea of forgiving someone more than once and is told to forgive 'seventy times seven', meaning endlessly (Mt 18:21). In the biblical story that follows this, it is clear that forgiveness is part of the relationship with God, that we reflect out that same forgiveness to others. The Lord's Prayer has the phrase 'forgive us our sins, as we forgive those who sin against us'. This is personally challenging today. In the culture of Jesus' day, where there were sin offerings and sacrifices to be bought and made in the temple, it challenged the whole religious and political system.

Jesus goes to God in prayer for love and strength, regularly taking time with God in the mountains. The account of the events in the Garden of Gethsemane shows Jesus wrestling in prayer to obey God's will, as though God does require Jesus to die. However, I think this is a consequence of staying with God's will for a way of relating that is loving and non-violent. Both Walter Wink and Steve Chalke write about the way this non-violent message of Jesus has been hidden, and I found their ideas illuminating when I first encountered them.[26]

Jesus teaches a non-violent way for the poor and downtrodden to respond and no longer accept humiliation. As one example, look at the phrase 'turn the other cheek'. Today this has come to mean the acceptance of something unpleasant done to you. Scholars have shown how far this is from Jesus' intention though. In his culture, where issues of honour and shame were behind much of behaviour, a superior would slap someone inferior with the back of their right hand on the right cheek as a humiliation. But if the person then turned their left cheek, the person would now have to hit them with the palm of their right hand, the hit of an equal.

'Going the extra mile' is a phrase we interpret as meaning

helping more than has been asked for (Mt 5:41). But in Jesus' day, for a Jew to go the extra mile would have got the Roman soldier in trouble, as he was legally entitled to require people to carry his pack for one mile only. So there was a subversive element to Jesus' teaching that was not about violent revolution, as the Zealots wanted, but about a peaceful challenge to the systems and structures that demeaned people. As Gandhi experienced, this does not mean you do not suffer violence from those you challenge. Jesus shows that living this non-violent way and truly loving enemies means that you give your life, in the last resort, rather than feed violence with violence – that this way, the Father's way, is the path to victory over evil. I find this very meaningful when I think about the cross, particularly as, for the first few hundred years of Christianity, Christians did not fight, and if they were soldiers when they converted, they either died a martyr's death or left the army. Only when Christianity became the state religion of Rome did the message change, when Augustine suggested that whilst it was wrong to kill others to protect yourself, you could do so to protect others. From this beginning came the requirements for the 'just war' theory. I sometimes wonder what the world would look like if Christians had continued to live by truly loving enemies.

Paul talks of Christ crucified being a stumbling block to Jews and a foolishness to Gentiles (foreigners) in his first letter to the Corinthians (1 Cor 1:23). The whole idea that the Messiah could suffer a shaming and humiliating death on a cross was incomprehensible at that time. To see God there was even more so, but that is the Christian claim. One of the ideas about the cross that resonate for me is that on the cross we see God alongside us in suffering. I find it a helpful view of the cross when struggling with illness myself, and I know others do too, or when confronted with some of the really difficult situations of living. Jesus knows what it is to suffer and die, knows the human condition, so that whatever we face, Jesus is beside us.

Of course Jesus' suffering was not caused by illness, but by his obedience to God the Father, and the reaction to that by the religious and political people of his day. At one very simple level, Jesus' death is a political consequence of a religious system wanting to remove a threat to its authority. I was confronted by this understanding of suffering during the time the Church of England wrestled with whether women could be priests. I felt strongly called by God to serve as a priest but could not, as women were not allowed to be ordained as priests at that time. The insight I gained one Holy Week, into suffering as a consequence of following God's will, was profound and strengthening.

I still struggle with the sacrificial ideas, hymns and pictures of Jesus on the cross, particularly when we talk of Jesus being sacrificed for sin. They are naturally disturbing anyway. I can see it was very meaningful for the early church, which was accustomed to ritual sacrifice as part of the way of worshipping God, to see Jesus' death in this way. I recognise that sacrifice can also be about making something holy (that is the origin of the word 'sacrifice': to make sacred), and in church we have, as part of prayer, the phrase 'a sacrifice of praise', so it is not all cruel.

Exploring biblical ideas of sacrifice during a period of study one time, it occurred to me that the sacrifice of the lambs at Passover was not the sin-offering of the time, not a sacrifice for receiving forgiveness. The Passover commemorates the events leading to the escape of the Israelites from slavery in Egypt. My research revealed that the sacrifice of lambs at Passover was a very ancient ritual called an apotropaic sacrifice, for protection against evil. Somehow for me this makes what happens on the cross much bigger and more cosmic than my sin being forgiven, though I am grateful for that too. The cross is complex, and no one view of it is sufficient for all that it conveys. Christ, the Son of God crucified! It is equally both shocking and a gift that is so central to Christian worship.

The crucified God. As if God says, 'The buck stops here. I take responsibility for all of creation, all the trouble that freewill causes when people make bad choices. I, God, take responsibility, show the true way of great love; and in response to the cross I give you resurrection, the transformative powers of resurrection in your life now, if you choose to accept it.' We would know nothing of Jesus' death on the cross without the Resurrection; without that he might just be known as a Jewish teacher or prophet of long ago. It is the Resurrection that puts the life, the teaching and the Way of Jesus on the world stage.

For many, gazing at and meditating on the cross transcends all the ideas and thinking about it, as it is an experience that speaks to the heart and soul. From this experience many cultures have created their own image of Jesus on the cross. I collect such images as they all tell us something more about the effect the cross has, and how people identify with it. From a passive, straw image from Asia; the black African wearing red; an agonised South American cross, made of nails, with its scream of agony; to the long-faced European Jesus, often very beautifully arranged on the cross, Jesus is imaged so that different peoples identify with him. There are many more of course, as people see themselves there. This was even more explicit when Christas were created: a cruciform female figure, or actually on the cross. The Toronto Christa inspired a beautiful poem by a woman who, when she gazed at the cruciform woman, saw her experience of rape in a different way. The cross touches deep places within, so that just being with the cross is to recognise the presence of God in the depths of our own experience. Maybe that is enough.

The tomb area

As you walk through the mirror doors from the Passion Garden, the path takes you through a broken-down tomb. It is necessarily a broken-down tomb as it would have been unsafe to make a cave-type tomb. We did not want to avoid the death of Jesus, and that he was buried. So to get to the Resurrection Garden, you have to walk through the tomb and the reality of death. Here, still using the black, quiet, recycled tyres as the path, there is a pause. There is a slab where the body could have been laid, and the plants at the side have black flowers or leaves, except for the poppies, in due season, as they are so reminiscent of death in war. We have grown ivy on the walls, as ivy is for faithfulness in the language of flowers. Here we see it as God the Father's faithfulness to Jesus, and Jesus' faithfulness to the Way of God.

This is the place where I have occasionally been asked, 'So did Jesus die here then?' Younger primary-school children, having passed the life-size cross and standing in a broken tomb get caught up in the story. A teacher told me how valuable it was to her to have the story in a picture form, giving her a different way to talk about it.

In the Ignatian Exercises the 'tomb day' is a pause between the difficult meditations on the Passion of Jesus, with all the inner spiritual disturbance and sadness this can cause, and the joy of the Resurrection.

Your death, Lord Jesus,
changed everything.
A fearful future
and deep sadness
filled us as we hid.

Gone, the excitement
of being with you.
Challenging confusion,
now lost darkness,
empty misery.

And we wait,
faith, a faint flicker,
hope, a dying ember,
love, a dark flame.
We wait, not knowing
what tomorrow will bring.[27]

The Resurrection Garden

This is the last garden area on this Ignatian journey. Here visitors are invited to ponder on the resurrection of Jesus, what that means for us in our lives today, at our death, and in our aim, as the Exercises suggest, to find God in all things. We have tree-planting as the environmental idea here, and there are various symbols of resurrection to reflect on.

The first area of the Resurrection Garden, we call the Mary Garden, as the first experience of the Resurrection was Jesus' appearance to Mary Magdalene when she was weeping outside the tomb thinking Jesus' body had been stolen. As you come out of the tomb there is a large stone slab lying on the ground to the left, to recall the stone that had been rolled away from Jesus' tomb. The stone lies under the branches of an *ailanthus altissima* tree, the common name of which is tree of heaven. This tree was in the garden when we came, and this part of the journey was planned round its position.

Under the tree in early spring there is a carpet of snowdrops. On the other side of the path is a bed of rose bushes, one of which is the Mary Magdalene rose. The fragrance of this rose resembles myrrh, so the growers presumably connected Mary Magdalene to the unnamed woman (whom the Bible refers to as 'a sinner') who anointed Jesus' feet with a pot of myrrh. Or else, they may have confused her with Mary of Bethany, the sister of Martha, who was overwhelmed with gratitude for the healing of her brother Lazarus from death, and in response anointed and washed Jesus' feet. Mary of Bethany is in fact the only named woman to wash and anoint Jesus' feet (Jn 12:3).

Maybe it is not surprising that rose-growers made this mistake, since historically the Church itself has conflated Mary Magdalene and the unnamed woman called a sinner who anointed Jesus' feet in Luke's Gospel. You will not find Mary Magdalene named as a 'sinner' anywhere in the Bible; she had been healed by Jesus of seven demons. Elsewhere in the gospels, when people are healed of demons, they were probably suffering from what we would today recognise as mental illness. Mary Magdalene clearly travelled with the disciples who followed Jesus, and was the first to see and talk with the risen Christ.

The Mary Garden has living willow posts around it, giving an open but enclosed feel to the area. The path is yellow brick. At the centre of the Mary Magdalene area is an almond tree, actually the third we have tried to grow. We are really too far north and too high up for almond trees to be happy. However in Greek it is called *amygdalia*, and linked with Mary Magdalene for the sound of the name. This area also has plants that have an attractive smell, including: an alpine mint bush, a winter-flowering honeysuckle and a small chamomile lawn in front of a bench. The plants are white, yellow or pale pink, colours of spring here in the UK that always speak of life returning after winter. We always have a few garden tools here, as Mary mistook the risen Jesus for a gardener.

As you walk further into the Resurrection Garden the path changes from yellow brick to yellow Breedon gravel. The hedge round the whole Resurrection Garden is beech, which has the amber autumn leaves remaining on the plant till the new spring growth appears. With the Mary Garden we had told the biblical story, and so thought the remainder of this garden would be the easiest to do. In fact we were really stuck. A friend of mine, writing a book, had a similar experience; he left the chapter on resurrection till last because he thought it would be the easiest to write, but then found it the hardest. So did we. Ideas had flowed easily for all the other areas, and it struck me that as Christians we celebrate Lent and Easter Day, then stop and give little or no attention to the great fifty days of Easter, and barely acknowledge Pentecost unless there is a charismatic influence. After much thought, prayer and debate we decided to do symbols of resurrection.

The first place is a storytelling area, since we all have resurrection stories but we just don't always recognise them as such. This area has two benches facing each other, on a paved base, underneath a hazel tree. Tiles with an interweaving pattern are part of the base – interweaving because resurrection joy is not a bubbly party joy, it is a joy that comes when God puts a different pattern on a difficult or painful experience. We have hung the pergola here with butterflies. Some of these are made from the broken glass of bottles thrown at Israeli tanks as they rolled through Bethlehem. The pieces of glass were collected and made into butterflies by craftspeople from the Palestinian social enterprise Hadeel, as a prayer for resurrection in their land.[28] Other butterflies were given to us by visitors who appreciated this idea.

The Resurrection Garden

The hazel tree is one in the garden, along with a hornbeam and another hazel, that we partly coppice in the traditional way. Coppicing is an old way of having fuel, and where we used to live in Hertfordshire you could see the remains of coppice woods with their thick, many-branched trunks. Coppice woods were the fuel for a village, one seventh being cut each year. The trees grew again, so by the eighth year the cycle repeated. The perpetual cutting and growing made, with the changes in light, for very different flora in the wood. Cut the tree and it comes again, like 'cut me down and I leap up high' in the song 'Lord of the dance',[29] by Sydney Carter – it seems an appropriate symbol for resurrection.

A little further along the path is a small peace garden. A gentleman I used to visit had half a cannonball shell in his garden that he used as a birdbath. It had been fired over Lichfield Cathedral during the English Civil War. When he died his daughter gave it to me for the garden. Building on the 'swords into ploughshares' idea (Micah 4:3) John made three wooden rifles, and we balanced the heavy cannonball shell on the tripod they made. Underneath is a circular rainbow of tiles that was made for us by a youth group. The rainbow is often used as a symbol of peace and we felt that peace would be a resurrection transformation for the world. Around the peace symbol we have planted a peace rose, and a very vigorous rose called the Angel of Lichfield. On the other side of the path is a small tree nursery, representing the environmental idea for this garden, because of the way trees clean the air and promote life. Trees from here have been given to many people, planted along a canal bank being restored locally and on the campsite next door to us.

A little further on the path, and you see two streams coming down the bank from a small pool at the top into a pool at the bottom. There is a wide variety of yellow and white planting

here, and we made it for a glory factor. Standing facing the path is a statue of Jesus, who could be gardening there. An oak tree was blown down on the campsite and we were allowed to take a section of trunk. A friend, Richard, soaked this in resin and carved the statue for us. We had said to leave the face blank for people to put their own interpretation on. However, when Richard was carving he stood the wood in his prayer corner for reflection when not working on it. He came to us with a sheepish expression and the statue well-wrapped. Gazing at the wood, he had seen a face in the grain, all he did was to expose the pattern of the grain. The carving has its own presence.

I grow wheat here, although it's not the best growing place for it, but in Paul's letters he uses the ear of wheat and growth of seeds as a resurrection example (1 Cor 15:36–38). Somewhere around either this space or the Mary Garden there is St John's Wort. It is a herb that moves about, and is known for its properties to cure depression. Apparently St Columba used to put a sprig in his armpit at times. An aid for depression seems very appropriate for this garden, resurrection bringing joy and transformation.

There is a detour from the main path here, which leads to a meditation hut at the highest point of the garden. Quite by chance it faces dawn at Easter time, one of the unplanned coincidences that seem very right. The hut is hexagonal. The base is made of recycled plastic. The sides were meant to be growing willow, but little of that took here, however the hedges of the garden seem adequate. It is a sheltered and hidden place to sit, facing a small pool. It was in this pool that we spotted a great crested newt, which confirmed that we have three kinds of newts in the garden, with no effort on our part.

The resurrection garden ends with a small Holy Spirit area, with twirlies to catch the slightest breeze, and white doves, cut out from a white, powder-coated copper sheet, fixed to the gate.

There is a wayside box on a post, of the type that is often seen on the continent where someone has had an accident, or to give thanks that someone survived an accident. These generally have flowers, candles and religious pictures in them. Ours has a sand tray for visitors to light a candle as a prayer when they leave this garden. You are then back at the beginning, reminiscent of the lines from T.S. Eliot's poem *Four Quartets*:

'We shall not cease from exploration,
And the end of all our exploring
Will be to arrive where we started
And know the place for the first time
Through the unknown remembered gate ...' [30]

The spiritual journey never ends. The Ignatian idea is that you would travel on and see God in all things.

Resurrection,
life beyond death?
Hope fulfilled,
beyond hope's expectation?
Mind-blowing, confusing,
I am struck to silent tears
at the possibility;
words stuck in my throat
at the awesomeness;
stilled in disbelief
at the reality –
of you –
Jesus.

Rabbouni!

The environmental idea in the Resurrection Garden

I grew up in the East End of London just after the Second World War. We were near the docks, though I never saw the water, just the back of the warehouses. It was/is one of the poorest areas of London, where the latest group of immigrants came to Britain to start their stay, and where the housing was crowded and of poor quality. Every winter there would be smog, a thick yellow fog that was made impenetrable by the level of industrial pollution, the effects of burning coal and the vehicle emissions that were mixed with it. As my sister and I walked back from school we would tie a hanky over our noses. By the time we were home it would be black. The dreadful smog of 1952 caused some 4000 deaths directly, and is thought responsible for a further 8000 deaths in the following months. It led to the first Clean Air Act which, among other legislative requirements, stipulated that chimneys had to be built higher and that only smokeless fuel could be burned in certain areas.

These smogs have largely gone since the various Clean Air Acts were enforced. Los Angeles has also cleaned up its polluted air, but in Beijing people wear masks to give some protection from the bad air.

We know that a number of diseases and conditions, like lung diseases and asthma, are made worse by breathing bad air and that it contributes to a reduced ability to resist disease in general. We have also discovered that not all bad air, like nitrogen oxide (nox) and particulate matter (PMs), can be seen and smelt.

Dr Xand van Tulleken ran an experiment to show the damage in Kingsheath, Birmingham.[31] He did a range of health tests on himself after breathing filtered air in a special suit; then ran the same tests after breathing the air in Kingsheath High Street for three hours. The tests showed that he had higher blood pressure and that his brain was a bit slower from the time in the High Street. Prolonged exposure to bad air could affect brains, thicken blood, inflame arteries and lungs, cause strokes and heart attacks and make an asthma attack more likely, he concluded. With thermal cameras he and his team revealed the fumes from the vehicles in the High Street and outside the primary school, and the driving behaviours that made them worse.

Working with local people, Dr. Xand and his team set out to show that the air could be improved in just one day. To do this they introduced a large hedge in tubs at the edge of the pavement, to help filter pollution, and had no parking in the High Street, to the consternation of some businesses. Many of the children had a walking bus instead of their parents driving them to school. (A walking bus is where children walk together in twos, with a few adults beside them organising crossing roads and directions.) The team also involved the local council to get the traffic lights in sync, so that when you went through one set of lights you also went through the next, instead of stopping and starting. All this succeeded by reducing nox by 20% and PMs by 30% outside the school, with almost the same reduction in the High Street. The discoveries we make may create challenges, but have the capacity to transform our lifestyle and heal the damage we cause.

In the early 1990s the idea of planting Community Forests to enhance the environment and clean the air was funded and promoted for ten forest areas in England.[32] They are all near built-up areas; one is near where we live now, thirty miles north of Birmingham in the Cannock area, and another where we used to live, near St Albans, some twenty miles north of London, and there is a swathe of Community Forests across the north of England near Manchester, Liverpool and Newcastle. Over the years, 10,000 hectares of new woodland has been planted and 27,000 hectares of existing woodland brought under management. With substantial voluntary help from the public, hedges have been created or improved and foot and cycle paths restored. Leisure space and enhanced quality of life are two of the aims of Community Forests, and it is the largest environmental regeneration project in England. Each Community Forest works in partnership with local authorities, other local and regional partnerships, the Forestry Commission and Natural England. The founding basis for each forest is a government-approved Forest Plan, a 30-year vision of landscape-scale improvement.

Trees also have great potential in a bio-economy. In Finland there is a large processing plant in which everything that is usually made from oil is instead made from wood and plants. For example, they have replaced plastic packaging, both tray and film, with packaging made from cellulose, which can also be used to make textiles. If you have viscose or rayon as the materials for your clothes, this could already have come from cellulose. The factory uses everything that comes from the tree. Even the sludge is used, to make bio-gas for cars, so they have 100% zero waste.[33]

Trees improve air quality; they also improve soil quality and affect climate. Senegal in West Africa has a hot, tropical climate with a rainy season and a dry season. During the rainy season, between the months of July and September, there is generally between 100-500mm of rain, but less rainfall is being recorded now. The rest of the year is dry with a hot, dry, strong wind blowing from the desert (the north of the country is half desert). The wind blows away the good soil, which makes it hard for crops to grow. There were serious droughts in 1972 and 2002. After independence from France in 1960, the government allowed people to cut down trees to make charcoal. This meant that whole forests were destroyed.[34] And now, because the trees have gone and the animals eat up all the grass and plants faster than they grow, more and more of the land is turning into desert. Farmers now find it very hard to earn a living and families often do not have enough to eat. Some of the older people remember a time when the land looked very different. Houleymata Diallo, 60, says, 'As time has gone by, the trees have gone.' Abdoulaye Noliaye, 57, was a farmer before the trees were chopped down and the droughts came. He thinks that more of the land is turning to desert. 'The desert gives us lots of sun, causing lots of wind to blow, taking all the nutrients from the soil.' He is now president of a local group that works to protect the earth. Christian Aid helps the group learn how to plant and care for trees, to increase the tree cover where they can.[35]

On average, each person in Senegal emits 0.4 tonnes of CO_2 a year; compare this figure to the UK and Ireland average figures, 9.4 tonnes and 10.3 tonnes respectively. These and other dryland areas of the world are home to about 2 billion people, the vast majority among the world's poorest people.

In Niger, and in other places in Africa, they are now practising farmer-managed natural regeneration (FMNR). Tony Rinaudo of World Vision worked in Niger as resident expert from the 1980s; he watched one farmer friend plant his crop three times, both of them knowing each crop would fail for lack of rain, as it had the previous year. Niger has only a four-month opportunity for rain. Crows, locusts and other insects made it even harder to grow enough food for families, or to have enough fodder for animals.

In despair of ever bringing improvement to the area, Tony prayed for help, acknowledging the way the land had been wrecked. Then, for the first time, he noticed stumps, like clumps of desert grass, but actually an 'underground' forest, just waiting for the chance to grow. Like coppicing in England, these trees were there but cut and uncared for.

To begin with, it was hard to convince farmers that leaving trees in their fields and looking after them would increase their crop yields. Attitudes to the land had to be challenged and some laws changed; but it was eventually shown that care for the tree stumps and allowing them to regenerate brought shelter and humus to the soil, created habitat; and wildlife returned – spiders, lizards, birds, amongst others, creating a better natural balance. With a cheap knife, farmers learned to prune the stumps that used to be cut and burned every year, to allow the trees to grow. Within three years they had more tree poles for building, firewood and selling. They could hang beehives in the trees. With the trees came fruit – some that had not been seen for generations; there was also more fodder for the animals. There was a significant difference in the resistance to drought. And now, as farmers have talked to other farmers, 500 million hectares have been regenerated. Over twenty years 200 million new trees have grown, 500,000 tons of cereal a year is grown – and 2.5 million people are better off.[36]

Tony has now been working at this regeneration of forests for many years and has seen old men weep at the return of fruits they had not eaten since childhood. It is a resurrection project that has benefited so many people and benefited the environment. You can listen to Tony's lectures on You Tube (search for 'Reversing desertification in arid and semi-arid lands').

With space technology, scientists have discovered that there are trees equivalent to another Amazon forest in the dry lands, but looking very different from the forests of wetter areas of the planet. The trees are more widely spaced and often in small clusters.

In North America, in northern Indiana, Gene Stratton-Porter wrote in the early years of the 20th century of the climate changing. It is the first mention of climate change that I have ever read. Farmers were cutting trees and draining the swamp in the Limberlost area that she loved, and she noticed how this was changing the climate: less rain, the lakes lower, and the birds she loved no longer came to the area. She used her wealth to buy 120 acres there to save some of the natural environment so that there could be some space left for the wildlife of the region. People can still visit the site with her log cabin and the nature reserve.[37]

Our very small tree nursery represents the possibilities for a healthier, better life for people, the air and the land. A resurrection way.

The thinking behind the Resurrection Garden

The resurrection of Jesus is central to the Christian gospel and the reason for Christianity growing as a faith, so it is worth looking at the information we are given. All the gospels agree that Jesus rose from the dead and was seen by some followers for a time. The details differ between authors, which may be an indication of authenticity or that the authors were choosing to emphasise aspects of the event that were of particular relevance to their intended readers. In summary the recorded appearances are:

In Mark, Matthew and Luke, the women note where Jesus is buried and go to the tomb early on Sunday morning with aromatic spices but find the tomb empty. Those named are Mary of Magdala, Mary the mother of James and either Salome or Joanna, but there is a clear suggestion there are other women. The stone is rolled away; in Matthew there is an earthquake. Angels, or a youth in white, tell the women that Jesus is risen and is going to Galilee; they are to go and tell the disciples. Jesus meets them as they go, and speaks to them. 'Don't be afraid, go and tell my

The Resurrection Garden   101

brothers to go to Galilee.' In Mark the women are too afraid to say anything; in Luke they tell the disciples, who dismiss it as nonsense. (Mk 16:1–8; Mt 28:1–10; Lk 24:1–9)

In Matthew, the eleven disciples go to Galilee and meet Jesus on a mountain and receive a commission from him to spread the gospel. We also learn in Matthew that the guards are paralysed with fright, and later are bribed by the chief priests to say the disciples stole Jesus' body at night. (Mt 28:16–end)

In Mark, there is a later ending where we learn that Jesus appears first to Mary of Magdala, who takes the news to the disciples but they don't believe her. Later he appears to two of them walking in the country; they take the news and again no one believes them. Jesus then appears to the eleven disciples when they are eating. Jesus reproaches them for their disbelief and gives them the commission to spread the gospel over the whole world. Jesus is then taken into heaven. (Mk 16:9–20)

In Luke's Gospel, we also have a full account of the walk to Emmaus. Two people walking sadly home from their stay in Jerusalem after Jesus was crucified, meet, but do not recognise, Jesus. In the conversation Jesus explains the scriptures to them and they invite him in for a meal. They recognise Jesus as he breaks bread, and Jesus vanishes from their sight. They then return to Jerusalem, where Simon has seen Jesus, and recount their own experience. Jesus appears among them and underlines his teaching. Jesus shows his wounds and eats fish to convince them he is not a ghost. He tells them to stay in Jerusalem until they have received the Father's gift. Jesus then leads them to Bethany, blesses them and is parted from them. (Lk 24:13–end)

In John's Gospel, we get further details. Mary of Magdala goes to the tomb early, presumably with other women as she says 'we' when later talking to the disciples. The stone has been moved and the tomb is empty. She runs to tell the disciples, and Peter and one other disciple (referred to as 'the one whom Jesus loved') run to the tomb, and find it is indeed empty, with the linen grave wrappings lying there, the cloth for Jesus' head folded separately. They leave and Mary stays, crying, and encounters Jesus, whom she at first mistakes for the gardener. She goes and tells the disciples. (Jn 20:1–18)

Later that evening Jesus appears to the disciples though their door is locked. They are joyful and Jesus breathes on them to receive the Holy Spirit. (Jn 20:19–23)

Thomas is not there, but is with them a week later when Jesus appears again, and invites him to put his hands in the wounds. Thomas says, 'My Lord and my God.' (Jn 20:24–29)

A second ending has Jesus appearing to some of the disciples, Simon Peter, Thomas, Nathaniel, the sons of Zebedee and two others, when they go fishing on the Sea of Tiberius. They catch nothing, but Jesus, from the beach, tells them to put the net on the other side of the boat – and they catch a great many fish. 'The disciple Jesus loved' says, 'It is the Lord'; Peter jumps in the water and swims ashore; the rest bring the boat in. Jesus has prepared breakfast, but they don't dare ask if he is Jesus. They eat. We are told that this is the third time Jesus has appeared to them. Peter has a conversation with Jesus, where he is asked, three times, how much he loves Jesus. Different Greek words for love are used: *agapeo*, unconditional love, and *phileo*, the love of a friend. Three times Peter is told to feed Jesus' sheep, possibly as a way to offer healing to Peter for the three times he denied Jesus. Jesus knew Peter would deny him, whereas Peter said he would die for Jesus (Jn:13:37), so this conversation has Peter acknowledging the reality of his love for Jesus. There is also a prophecy about Peter's death. (Jn 21:1–19)

Later, the author of the Book of Acts describes Paul's encounter with the risen Jesus on the road to Damascus (Acts 9:1–19). This would have been some considerable time after the experiences of the disciples, as the early Christians were already being persecuted. Also, in one of Paul's own letters, he describes the appearances of Jesus that he knows of, as part of his preaching and teaching in 1 Corinthians 15:3–11. These include: Jesus appearing to Peter; to the twelve; to five hundred followers at once, many of whom were still alive when Paul was writing; to James and all the apostles. Paul's letter is the earliest written account of the Resurrection.

As a child, Easter to me was a time of joy. I made Easter gardens on a plate, flowers were back in church and there were chocolate eggs. I delighted in this 'ending' to the story of Jesus in the gospels and the sense conveyed to me that Jesus was always with us. When I began to question the tenets of the Christian faith, and the possibility of resurrection in particular, I read *Who Moved the Stone?*, by Frank Morrison, and found him very convincing.

Over the years as I studied and reflected, I found that the most convincing evidence of the reality of the Resurrection for me was the change in the disciples after the Resurrection. Jesus would be a little-known Jewish teacher without the Resurrection and the deep change that made in those who followed him. After Jesus' dreadful death the disciples were a frightened group of people hiding behind locked doors. The Romans at that time would sometimes round up the followers of someone who had been crucified and crucify them as well, so they would have been in fear for their own lives. From the despair following Jesus' death, the disciples become people who travel the known world telling the story of Jesus, convincing others to join them in also becoming followers of Jesus. They face hardship, prison, floggings and death in order to spread the good news about Jesus, and to establish the way he taught them to live with each other. Others join them, know Jesus to be with them, and we hear in the letters of Paul and the Book of Acts of lives that are changed.

The early history of Christianity has inspired people down the centuries and still does today. In the letters of Peter, particularly 2 Peter 3, you can see that the early Christians clearly expected Jesus to return in their lifetime. In John 21:21–23 you can see an engagement with the reality that 'the disciple Jesus loved' was expected to live till Jesus' return. Some of Paul's advice about living makes sense when you realise that 'the day of the Lord' was expected to end life as they knew it, and establish life as Jesus taught. (As one example, see 1 Corinthians 7.) As the years pass and this manifestly does not happen, ideas shift and resurrection becomes generally a future expectation at death for those who follow Jesus. However, the experience of knowing Jesus in the present, knowing Jesus' voice, experiencing Jesus' presence, is a constant theme throughout Christian history. The Acts of the Apostles and the letters resound with the experience of his followers knowing Jesus still with them, the Resurrection having freed Jesus from time and space. Christians today would say the same.

I do believe there is something after death. I would never choose to detail what it would be like however. It is simply God's gift to us, and in faith I trust the deep love of God that it will be good. When taking a funeral I listen to people who talk of 'dad's just gardening up there' and other such comments. I have read good books where people imagine life after death, like C.S. Lewis' *The Last Battle*, or Mitch Albom's *The First Five People You Meet in Heaven*. They all project the life we know now, onto heaven. This can be a helpful way to reflect on the way we live now, but cannot describe the reality of life after death. As a baby in the womb I had no idea what life on earth would be like; the same is true of heaven.

When you reach this part of the Ignatian Exercises the grace you pray for at the beginning of each meditation changes, from the grace to suffer with Christ, to the grace to know joy, Easter joy. (A grace to the retreatant is a gift from God that comes through the meditations.) This joy is not so much a wild exuberance, but more like water on a sponge, something that permeates life and means that you see things from a different perspective. So it is an expectation that you would know something of the joy of the Creator in creation, and that a delight in creation would become a normal part of your experience. The aim is that you would know God in all things, and for many this awareness does come through the harder places of living.

The fundamental gift of resurrection now, as part of our daily life, is that we can know it in present time, know the transforming energy of resurrection as we struggle with the difficulties life brings. It would be an unusual life that had no sadness, hard painful situations or times when life seems overwhelmingly awful. For me it is meeting with Jesus in that very place of pain that releases a resurrection energy, if we are willing. In an earlier encounter in John's Gospel, Jesus meets Martha, sister to Mary of Bethany, just after their brother Lazarus has died. In the ensuing conversation Jesus makes it clear that to know him is to know the resurrection and the life now (Jn 11:23–27). I think we push resurrection to the past or future, unconsciously mostly, because we fear the consequences, the change from the comfortable rut we live in. Change is not easy, and the older you get the harder it is, so that sometimes it is only when life is awful that we are open to the possibility. Sometimes it is only those at the bottom of society's heap who are ready to work with change. Resurrection is costly, but we forget that whatever the comfortable rut, the struggle with change, the Easter that God wants to work in us is infinitely better. It is like life in brighter and sharper colours, like the tears of Mary Magdalene turning to joy, like the fields in Niger producing abundant food after the practices that were part of drought conditions, so of course it alters our lives, but for the good, so that we know life in all its abundance.

My favourite Easter hymn is an old one which starts 'Now the green blade riseth'. There is a phrase in it that can bring me to tears of both sadness and joy. 'When our hearts are wintr'y, grieving or in pain, Thy touch will call us back to life again.' The Easter message of resurrection takes the hard and difficult places in our lives and sets a new pattern on them. This is not to deny the hardship or the awfulness of what has happened; Jesus really did die that dreadful death and he was not resuscitated to live as we do and die later at a ripe old age. What the Resurrection did was to show us the cross in a new light, so we call the day of Jesus' death Good Friday, Easter making a new pattern and revealing the new creation.

Occasionally, when I am taking a person round the gardens, someone will tell me their resurrection story, as we stand somewhere in the Resurrection Garden. During my ministry I have walked alongside many people who have found new life after a desperate time; I have experienced that kind of resurrection myself. The kinds of things that are shared are both personal and social.

Illness, life-threatening, chronic and life-changing, is a common place where people experience the resurrection energy of God. It is not necessarily that the illness disappears, but that, in the difficulty of it all, some new life, a different energy or direction, comes and makes a difference. For some, God is alongside them in a new and close way that gives them an ability to live with a situation they would rather not be in. For others there is a change of life and the plans they have to let go of give way to a life-giving, fresh direction. I know some of this myself from living with a chronic disease that has a number of difficult social consequences. I know that the work I have done is different from that work I expected to do before I was ill, but that there has been, and is, life in its fullness in the work I grew into. I also know there were times when the awareness of God beside me carried me through the day, and graced times when the prayer of others blessed me. It is of course true that many who live with, or suddenly face, illness just have a horrible and difficult time, but there is another story that is true also.

That awful time when you are told you will be made redundant is another place where resurrection can be seen. I have known people weighed down and depressed by such news, but also known those who come alive in a different way from before and have gone on to live more fully than previously. I have even heard of someone who thanked his employers for making him redundant as he could see he needed the adventure of change.

Relationships, and especially family relationships, are another place where the resurrection energy can be recognised. What seems like a hopeless struggle with a difficult family member, or a relationship that has just got tangled up in a damaging way, these are places where life-giving change can be experienced. Jesus breathed his life into his followers, and in the same way, the transforming energy of his Spirit can be part of our lived experience now, way before our death.

Death and bereavement is, naturally, something we all experience. The death of someone we love can be a sad and lonely place and grief is a normal part of human life. The death of children is about the hardest place I know, that hole in the family, ever present. It is also true that in bereavement some can experience a resurrection surprise for themselves that would have come no other way. Death and dying is also a holy space, and those whose work is in hospitals or hospices have told me of an awareness of something inexplicable, an otherness, that has affirmed their belief in life after death.

I also believe it is not just in personal issues that resurrection can be seen, but in societal ones also. Many struggles for change in the way society has ordered itself are costly and painful. I was involved in the struggle to enable women as priests in the Church of England, a painful and difficult struggle, and I well recall the resurrection moment of walking through the archway of St Albans Abbey to the swelling music of the organ, as the first women in the St Albans diocese were about to be ordained as priests. Added to that moment were all the events of that day and celebrating communion for the first time in a crowded church, as there were so many for whom this was also a time of longed-for change. The birth of organisations like the United Nations and the European Union was part of the resurrection energy, I believe, since it offers the possibility for cooperation and peace between countries.

Resurrection can also be seen in our relationship to the earth that sustains us. We now know of considerable environmental change and the damage that is happening in many places and to many species. The struggle to alter ways of doing things, to stop damaging practices and to find ways to live that care for the environment are all part of the desire to live in right relationship. That is being on the side of resurrection.

So look for and notice where this resurrection energy is in your life and in the lives of those around you. It is worth praying and working for. Our culture in the West is so quick to tell the awful and to point out all that is wrong, and there is plenty to tell. Therefore the need for people to notice, work with and welcome the transforming energy of Easter, and to point to that, is all the greater. Tell the good news that Easter is real and can be experienced now in many aspects of our lives.

After the awesome moment,
the joy and gladness,
the discussions
and trying to make sense
of resurrection,
and the invitation;

then comes the living of it;
each day, each year,
to notice you, Living God,
in all that is about me,
add my mite
to your almighty?

Welcome Holy Spirit,
her wisdom, her presence,
the secret mystery
that nudges me along;
blind alone,
with you, is vision.

Comments from the Gardens visitors' book

'A thing (place) of beauty is a joy forever.' I thank God for the blessing and beauty of your shared vision and for sharing the fruits of all your hard labour. It is holy ground. WV

Thank you so much for your loving unobtrusive hospitality, for sharing the peace of this place, for the gardens, which have helped me open up to God's love and compassion. AB

For calm and the beauty of creation. For space to find the still point and come closer to God, I thank you. FE

A perfect place to be challenged, to wrestle and to be still, to just come as you are. HL

Wonderful fellowship. Great place of reflection. Will bring the idea to Malaysia. JS

… the journey through the garden has started me on an internal pilgrimage … SM

The Hermitage and the gardens … have enabled these precious days to be a 'resting place' – a time of encouraging, uplifting and renewing encounter with God. BR

… this is a place where the hours expand and where I can touch infinity and be refreshed. DP

Space to know – once again – that we are loved. Space then bringing us to see where we go wrong. Space to re-create us for forgiven lives. AR

A special place that really makes Jesus come alive and be with you wherever you may wander. An opportunity to appreciate God's wonderful creation. A reminder that we need to be good gardeners and carers for all that he has done and made for us. (12/5/13)

A remarkable place that will forever be etched on my memory. AM

... my heart has been opened again to feel the love I once thought was lost in my life. Walking in the 'Galilee' section of the garden brought me back to spending time with my dad as a child hunting for newts. I hope the sanctuary takes me on the journey as fulfilling as this short time at the Hermitage. PB

Thank you, I've had a lovely day. The Reflection Gardens are amazing, so moving. I loved meeting Jesus in the Resurrection Garden! N

I'm overwhelmed by the peace and presence of God in this place. The Hermitage and gardens are truly 'thin' places. GY

Here I found what lies behind the rabbit-proof gate – true resurrection. A genuine life-affirming (and life-changing) experience. Thank you for sharing God's goodness in such a lovely way. H (2/9/17)

I appreciate and congratulate you for listening to the heart of God – by creating a place – a 'Sanctuary' – for people to spend time with God. I am so refreshed and empowered. SI

I would probably fill half this [visitors'] book if I were to write all my feelings, reflections and conversations with God over these past few days. C (3-6/1/18)

Thank you for a wonderful day. The gardens are simply beautiful ... So many parts really spoke to me and the peace was so refreshing. A (11/5/18)

The immediacy of the crucifixion dawned on me. Never before has it struck me how traumatic it would have been for Mary and the others. MF

Prayer

St Ignatius Loyola (1491–1556)

Teach us, good Lord, to serve thee as thou deservest,
to give and not to count the cost;
to fight and not to heed the wounds;
to toil and not to seek for rest;
to labour and not to ask for any reward,
except that of knowing that we do thy will. Amen.

Appendix

Next steps: An environmental action activity for church groups

This activity can be completed in about 45 minutes and is suitable for any church group, for example the church council (or equivalent), a Mothers' Union, a men's breakfast group, or a youth group. Divide your group into sets of 4 or 5 people, and the activity is best done with each set sitting round a small table.

The following pages contain suggestions for environmental action under four headings; some of these may not be relevant to your situation, for example your church may not have any grounds, so you would leave those suggestions out. Photocopy the pages and cut them up so that each suggestion is on a small single piece of paper. Give each small group about 15–20 minutes for each of the suggestions – if you have a large group, you will need multiple copies of the suggestions so that some of the small groups will have the same suggestions and you have one or two spare batches. It is best to keep the suggestions in each subject area together so that you know which blocks of suggestions you have given to each small group.

When everyone is sitting comfortably, explain that you are giving them each a list of suggested environmental actions and their task is to make four piles:

– Our church is doing this already
– We can do this
– We might be able to do this
– This is not something we could do, or would be appropriate for us

and then to select (say) three from the 'can do' pile as the most suitable.

The last page of this appendix has a list of these categories and what people have to do, which you can photocopy and give to each small group.

Check that everyone understands what they are to do, hand out the packs of suggestions and the category lists and tell them to get on with it. Sometimes people will try to avoid starting by asking questions about detail – just tell them to do the best they can! Most people will be keen to engage in the activity and just get stuck in.

Our experience is that the small groups will work at different speeds, and one or two of them will finish quite quickly whilst others will spend a long time discussing some of the suggestions. You can give one of the spare packs of suggestions to the early finishers – checking that they are different from the ones they have already classified.

When everyone has finished, ask each small group to read out their 'top three'. You can either tick these off from a master copy of the suggestions (asking them for the letter/number code will help you to identify them quickly) or collect in all of the favoured suggestions. The final step is to get the whole group to agree (say) four things that they could do and decide who will be responsible for each one and report back at the next meeting. Exactly how you would want to do this will depend on the nature and structure of the group but it is important to capture the commitment at this moment when there will be enthusiasm around.

Lists of suggestions follow:

W = Worship and teaching
B = Buildings
L = Land
E = Global engagement
S = Community

W

W1. Suggest that the church has special Sundays relating to caring for God's earth (e.g. Creation Time, Environment Sunday, Rogation Sunday, etc.).

W2. Suggest that hymns and songs (and liturgies if used) in our church services are chosen to enable us to celebrate God's creation.

W3. Include environmental issues in prayers.

W4. Ask for caring for God's earth to be mentioned regularly in sermons.

W5. Ask to have guest speakers from A Rocha UK or other Christian environmental organisations (e.g. Christian Aid, Tearfund, Green Christian, the John Ray Initiative ...) to talk about environmental issues.

W6. Help youth and children's work leaders to include caring for God's earth as a teaching theme.

W7. Suggest that caring for God's earth is used as a focus of small group study in the church.

W8. Find ways to have the church's communications (e.g. newsletters, service sheets, magazines, social media, etc.) include items relating to the theme of caring for God's earth.

W9. Encourage the leadership to make a formal commitment to working towards an Eco-Church Award or other defined environmental goal.

B

B1. Get someone to help measure the energy use and calculate the carbon footprint of our church building(s).

B2. Find out whether the electricity (and gas if appropriate) supplied to our church building(s) is generated from renewable resources and/or charged according to our supplier's 'green tariff'.

B3. Find out whether the water supply to our church premises is metered.

B4. Ask whether rainwater collection facilities could be installed and used on our church premises (e.g. for visitors to graves).

B5. Ask whether the toilet cisterns on our church premises are fitted with dual-flush buttons or other water-saving devices.

B6. Arrange for toilet tissue made from recycled paper to be used on our church premises.

B7. Arrange for the cleaning products used around our church building(s) to be environmentally friendly.

B8. Arrange for the disposables (e.g. paper cups and plates, etc.) used on our church premises to be biodegradable/recyclable, or not used at all.

B9. Find out what office paper is used for in our church and come up with suggestions about ways to use less.

B10. Look into arranging for our church administration to use recycled paper.

B11. Set up a scheme for refilling or recycling printer ink cartridges.

L

L1. Help to make the land at our church encourage native wildlife and plants (e.g. provision of bird boxes and feeders, butterfly-friendly shrubs, etc.).

L2. Suggest that the land at our church includes areas set aside for the growing of fruit and vegetables.

L3. Look into ways our church could set aside a small area for the provision of a community garden.

L4. Suggest that properly designed and managed composting facilities are available on our church premises.

E

E1. Organise events providing an opportunity for local people to engage with local leaders on local environmental issues (e.g. local MPs or Council leaders).

E2. Arrange for local environmentalists to speak in our services.

E3. Organise environmental awareness-raising events (e.g. film evenings).

E4. Organise and/or participate in a community clean-up project (e.g. local litter-pick).

E5. Experiment with using a car-share scheme for our meetings.

E6. Suggest ways that users of our church premises can be encouraged to minimise resource use (e.g. notices about turning off lights are displayed, etc.).

E7. Suggest that our church commits to pray for a specific overseas environmental project.

E8. Suggest that our church participates in the Tearfund/Cord 'Toilet Twinning' scheme: www.toilettwinning.org.

E9. Find out about the impact of climate change and environmental degradation on Mothers' Union communities elsewhere in the world and inform the congregation about this.

E10. Suggest that our church financially supports an environmental charity.

E11. Look into ways that more fair trade and/or ethically sourced goods, and locally grown/organic/animal-friendly foods, are used at church services and events.

E12. Make sure that any meals provided by the church include a vegetarian option.

S

S1. Suggest that our church appoints an individual or group to champion the cause of our church community becoming more 'green'.

S2. Arrange for members of our group to undertake a personal carbon footprint audit.

S3. Discuss ways in which our members can limit their waste by adhering to the principles of reduce, reuse, recycle.

S4. Plan activities and/or events that facilitate the recycling and/or reuse of goods (e.g. clothes swap events or 'give and take' schemes).

S5. Suggest that our church operates a communal Christmas and/or Easter card scheme among the congregation.

S6. Have a regular stall in church selling fair trade and/or ethically sourced goods.

S7. Support a regular item in our church newsletters/on our church website with lifestyle tips and advice on caring for God's earth.

Make a pile of the suggestions under these headings:

- Already doing
- Can do
- Might do
- Not suitable/appropriate

When you have finished, pick the three most suitable from the 'can do' pile.

John Polhill

Note:

The group activity was inspired by the Eco-Church questionnaire 'Eco-Church: An Arocha Project', 2018.

Acknowledgements

Writing about our gardens is a project I have long wanted to complete but I am very aware that it would not have been possible without the help and encouragement of others. So to my son David, who asked me how the writing was going every time we met, and then quietly knocked down my 'very good' reasons for not writing, thank you. When my son Gary heard us talking about the project one time, he grinned at me and promised a text every day from his phone. The irritation of this text, coming regularly at 2pm, did provoke me into writing just so I could send a positive answer. So thank you to Gary. Without John's contribution I would have had even more reasons for not writing, but he would regularly say, 'I'll do the accounts, or the washing-up', or any number of things, 'you get on with writing'. Thank you, John. Why was I so resistant when I really *did* want to write about the gardens and our ideas? It is just one of life's puzzles.

Then a big thank you is due to those who read and commented, people giving another perspective is very helpful. So thank you to Ruth, Stephen, John, David, Alison and Kareen, and to Bishop Mike for his commendation. Last but not least, thank you to Neil of Wild Goose Publications for his considerate editing and to all the team at Wild Goose for their work.

Chris Polhill

Notes

1. www.nationalchurchestrust.org/explore/story/yew-trees
   www.bionity.com/en/news/1182277/scientists-discover-how-yew-trees-save-lives.html
2. www.bbc.co.uk/news/business-40198567
   https://en.wikipedia.org/wiki/Severn_Barrage
3. https://en.wikipedia.org/wiki/Renewable_energy_in_Germany
4. The book *Ask the Beasts: Darwin and the God of Love*, by Elizabeth A. Johnson, Bloomsbury, 2014, is an excellent exploration of science, Darwin and faith.
5. It is better to do the Spiritual Exercises than to read about them, but *Understanding the Spiritual Exercises*, by Michael Ivens SJ, Gracewing, 1998, is a helpful read.
6. www.ncbi.nlm.nih.gov/pmc/articles/PMC4874413
7. https://unearthed.greenpeace.org/2017/08/03/indonesia-forest-fires-begin
8. www.upcbarcodes.com/barcodes-demystified
9. www.rivercottage.net/campaigns
10. https://www.facebook.com/LoveFoodHateWasteCommunity
11. https://en.wikipedia.org/wiki/Water_resources
12. https://wcponline.com/2017/08/17/sustainable-water-management-singapore-water-story
13. *Revelations of Divine Love*, Mother Julian of Norwich, 13th Revelation
14. *The Enneagram: The Only Introduction You'll Ever Need*, by Karen Webb, Thorsons, 1996, is a very approachable book. The Jesuits developed this ancient tool for today's use.
15. *Nudge: Improving Decisions about Health, Wealth and Happiness*,

by Richard H. Thaler & Cass R. Sunstein, Penguin, 2009

16. To read more about Li Tim-Oi's life: www.ltof.org.uk/litimoi-story

17. Sermons of Columbanus, Sermon 1, an appendix in *The Eagle and the Dove: The Spirituality of the Celtic Saint Columbanus*, by Katherine Lack, Triangle, 2000
And on the Internet at https://celt.ucc.ie//published/T201053/index.html

18. www.ridinglights.org

19. https://practicalaction.org/news-media/2021/05/10/floating-gardens

20. https://www.christianaid.org.uk

21. https://practicalaction.org

22. https://www.christianaid.org.uk/site-search?search_api_fulltext=-climate+change

23. Desmond Tutu, 'We Fought Apartheid. Now Climate Change Is Our Global Enemy', *The Guardian*, September 20, 2014

24. www.chinadialogue.net/article/show/single/en/5193-Decline-of-bees-forces-China-s-apple-farmers-to-pollinate-by-hand

25. Walter Wink, *The Powers That Be, Theology for a New Millennium*, Chapter 4, Bantam Doubleday Dell, new edition, 2000

26. Walter Wink, *The Powers That Be*; Steve Chalke & Alan Mann, *The Lost Message of Jesus*, Zondervan, 2004; for in-depth theology, Walter Wink, *Engaging the Powers*; *Unmasking the Powers*; *Naming the Powers*, Augsburg Fortress Publishers

27. From *A Heart for Creation*, edited by Chris Polhill, Wild Goose Publications, 2010

28. www.hadeel.org

29. Copyright 1963 Stainer & Bell Ltd. London, England

30. T.S. Eliot, *The Four Quartets*, Faber & Faber, 1943

31. www.birminghammail.co.uk/whats-on/whats-on-news/bbc2-documentary-highlight-pollution-kings-14131117

32. https://englandscommunityforests.org.uk

33. https://finland.fi/business-innovation/finnish-bioeconomy-making-amazing-future

34. https://www.christianaid.org.uk/our-work/where-we-work/senegal

35. https://www.christianaid.org.uk/resources/get-involved/crazy-climate-case-studies

36. www.youtube.com/watch?v=Dm_qlyvdZ_A
www.wri.org/blog/2015/07/how-ethiopia-went-famine-crisis-green-revolution
www.wvi.org/timor-leste/video/renew-land-fmnr-timor-leste

37. Gene Stratton-Porter, *Tales You Won't Believe*, Ch. The Last Passenger Pigeon, Doubleday, Page & Co., 1925

For more information, photos in colour, videos, or to visit the Reflection Gardens:

www.reflectiongardens.org.uk

Wild Goose Publications, the publishing house of the Iona Community established in the Celtic Christian tradition of Saint Columba, produces books, e-books, CDs and digital downloads on:

- holistic spirituality
- social justice
- political, peace and environmental issues
- healing and wellbeing
- innovative approaches to worship
- song in worship, including the work of the Wild Goose Resource Group
- material for meditation and reflection

Visit our website at
www.ionabooks.com
for details of all our products and online sales